Comanche Medicine Man

Kenneth Coosewoon's
Great Vision, Blue Medicine,
and Sweat Lodge Healings

Clifford E. Trafzer
Beverly Sourjohn Patchell
Ronald Ray Cooper

Published by Coyote Hill Press, Camano Island, WA

Cover Design by Robin S. Hanks

Layout & Design by Robin S. Hanks

First Edition, 2015

Printed in the United States

ISBN: 978-0-9912641-4-8 All rights reserved.

Contents

The authors respectfully dedicate this volume

To Kenneth, Rita, and Doraline
And to Indigenous Healers that continue the Tradition

Kenneth Coosewoon lives near a federal wildlife refuge that maintains several buffalo, a reminder of the old days and a former way of life. Comanche, Kiowa, and many Native Americans of the Great Plains considered buffalo or American bison, a sacred animal. Kenneth's Comanche and Kiowa relatives lived off the buffalo until hunters nearly exterminated the animals. In 1907, the New York Bronx Zoo sent fifteen buffalo to the Wichita Mountains. Today, the herd numbers 650 animals that roam free on a federal Wildlife Refuge of over 59,020 acres.

Buffalo Skull Vision
Fort Sill Indian School, 1978

"My grandson and I spent the night at the Fort Sill Indian School where I directed an alcohol and drug treatment center for American Indians. I got up that night and looked at a crack in a darkened window and saw a blue spark glowing in the darkness of the glass. It caught my eye and I watched it glow. As I watched it, the blue spark got brighter and brighter then changed into a buffalo skull. Then it turned into a strong, fierce looking American Indian man and I could see he had blue paint on four sides of his face on the forehead, cheeks, and chin. He looked strong and powerful. I could see his face real good and he had like small, stretched buffalo hides over part of his lower face but I could see his eyes. In the glass, he seemed to back up and fade into the blue spark and disappeared from my vision.

I thought the spirit was a good sign, but I did not know. So I smudged the darkened window with sage and cedar, asking Grandfather that if that was a good spirit to have it reappear, but if it was a bad spirit, to have it go away. We did not want or need that. I saw that spirit a few times. It is a good and powerful spirit."

Kenneth Coosewoon, March 1, 2015

Preface

On March 1, 2015, Kenneth Coosewoon retold the story of the buffalo skull vision he had at the old Fort Sill American Indian Boarding School in Lawton, Oklahoma. Plains Indian medicine people have long used the buffalo skull as part of their medicine ways, since the great animals played a central role their religions, histories, oral narratives, and ways of life. The story is just one of many that forms the life and times of Kenneth Coosewoon, a Comanche healer from Medicine Park, Oklahoma. While most people would call Kenneth a Medicine Man, he denies being a medicine man, saying "I don't know what a medicine man is." Kenneth once explained, "I don't know what to call myself. A lot of people say I'm a medicine man, but I'm no medicine man. Besides, I don't know what a medicine man is."

Coosewoon prefers the term "spiritual healer" or "holy man," saying, "I'm a spiritual man. I try to walk the Good Red Road." Coosewoon is a holy man, a spiritual leader, and Native healer that many people today would call a medicine man. He once explained, "in the old days we had a lot of medicine men. They were just like your doctors today . . . specialized in different things." Kenneth explained, "we had bone doctors and arrow or bullet doctors. We had birthing doctors and herb doctors. All the power came from Grandfather but these medicine men and women knew how to ask Grandfather for power and help, and it would come." Kenneth continues this tradition of healing, using prayer and many items to bring the healing power to people, including the pipe, sage, cedar, tobacco, eagle feathers, and buffalo skull. Like past healers commonly called Medicine Men in the English language, Kenneth Coosewoon received the gift of healing during his Great Vision from the Grandfather, his term for the Creator, God, Almighty, or the Supreme Being. And like many Medicine Men of the past, Kenneth uses his healing gift to help or heal people. He helps everyone that asks him for assistance, and he never discriminates between people, saying, "we are all the same, human beings, put here by the same Creator, and we all need help at times."

Kenneth Coosewoon is an extraordinary spiritual man who is quick to tell you that the power to heal comes from Grandfather, Great Spirit, Amahnawet, Namipiap, Impeeash, or whatever term you wish to use to describe the spiritual Creator of all things, animate and inanimate. He meets all the requirements for a Medicine Man known in Indian Country. He uses spiritual healing through the Sweat Lodge to cure people with physical, mental, or spiritual illnesses. He comforts and counsels the ill and dying. He prays to prevent disease or improve one's destructive behavior. He counsels troubled people. He asks the Grandfather to cure disease and ill health of all kinds. However, he never promises that his Ceremonies or prayers will heal anyone because, "that is in the hands of the Grandfather, not me." He only does what he is asked to do and that is help others. "The Grandfather told me to help others," Kenneth explained, "and that's what I do." Coosewoon conducts healing ceremonies through the Sweat Lodge Ceremony, and he often prays for people, smudging them with his eagle feathers and the smoke from sage, cedar, or sweetgrass. Kenneth tells people, "prayers are the most powerful things on earth," and "prayers never hurt anyone, so let's pray and see if the Grandfather will intervene and help you."

Coosewoon assists people to fight or cure physical, mental, and spiritual health problems. He lives his life in a holy way, following the Good Red Road. Kenneth attributes his ability to heal to the Grandfather, Creator, Supreme Being, or Great Spirit—not his own innate ability. Coosewoon believes that all the various terms used in Native and English for the Supreme Being are the same and that "God" or the Holy Healing Spirit has given him authority to use healing power to help other living things, including humans and animals. The three authors involved in this book have worked on this project with Kenneth, and each of us have seen him doctor people and animals. We have seen Coosewoon healing people, and we have watched him counsel people of all ages.

Independently, we have witnessed Coosewoon asking the Grandfather to alter the weather by changing the course of a tornado, sparing a geographical area of a massive thunderstorm, and altering the direction of a wild fire. In each of these cases, Coosewoon's prayers were answered in dramatic ways.

Since 1978 when Kenneth experienced his Great Vision and received his Blue Medicine, Coosewoon has used the powers given to him by the Master of Life to help others without compensation or expectations of payment, gifts, and any remuneration whatsoever. Unlike some indigenous healers that require payment, either through cultural customs or the economic realities of contemporary life, Kenneth never asks for payment. However, he would say, "I have been paid many times by seeing the healing." He has helped many people over a lengthy period of time and felt the joy of watching the renewal of health among hundreds of people.

Coosewoon is a humble and holy man who never boasts about his ability to help or heal others. He quite reluctantly allowed us to interview him to gain information for this volume. We have traveled with Kenneth when he has conducted ceremony and assisted as he helped others. He has gifted us with many revealing and captivating stories about his life, vision, and experience as a healer. He cannot remember all the people he has helped, as he kept no written records.

Ronald Ray Cooper is the grandson of Kenneth Coosewoon, and he grew up under the watchful eye and care of the Comanche healer. A Comanche himself, Ronald has spent his life learning from Kenneth and conducting healings with his Grandfather to help other people. Beverly Sourjohn Patchell is Cherokee/Creek from Oklahoma who met Kenneth as an adult and received the benefit of his healing before beginning her tutelage under Coosewoon. Over the years, she has been Kenneth's student and assisted him during healings, inviting many other health care practitioners into his world to learn a new way of thinking about and caring for those in need of healing. Clifford Trafzer, a man of Wyandot and German ancestry, met Kenneth through his friendship with Beverly Patchell and Rita Coosewoon. They met during a conference on American Indian medicine at the University of Oklahoma campus in Norman. The three authors have worked closely with Kenneth Coosewoon and offer their individual stories about Kenneth so they might open a window to understanding a contemporary Native American healer and one way in which a healer works today to help others through spiritual medicine.

We wish to thank many people that helped us create this work, especially Kenneth and Rita Coosewoon who gave of their time and knowledge to share many oral histories with us. We offer our sincere and deep appreciation to

Robin and Richard Hanks of Coyote Hill Press for copyediting and producing this volume. Their efforts have resulted in the production of a handsome volume. We are thankful for the suggestions provided during the review stage of production and we feel the work is much improved as a result of comments. We thank our families for giving us time to research and travel. Ronald wishes to thank Krystal and his extended family. Beverly thanks her family Jack, Jackson, Andrew, and Andrew, Jr. as well colleagues at the University of Utah and University of Oklahoma. Clifford thanks Lee Ann, Tess Nashone, Hayley Kachine, Tara Tsaile, Louise, Donna, Sally, Ron, and Alan. He also wishes to thank his colleagues at the University of California, Riverside, and beyond, including Kim Wilcox, Steve Cullenberg, James Sandoval, Shaun Bowler, Paul D'Anieri, Joshua Gonzales, James Fenelon, Robert Przeklasa, Randolph Head, Rebecca "Monte" Kugel, Michelle Raheja, Katherine Kinney, Jacqueline Shea Murphy, and Jason Weems.

Clifford E. Trafzer
Beverly Patchell
Ronald Cooper
March 1, 2015

Introduction
Coming Through A Fog: An Overview

During the first third of his life, Kenneth Coosewoon walked through a fog. With his first wife, Doraline, and with his daughters, Rae Lynn and Deanna, Kenneth walked through a fog. According to his second wife, Rita Coosewoon, Kenneth's family name in Comanche means "hard to see" or "it's like trying to see through a fog or cloud." Many Comanche people today think Coosewoon means "Gray Eyes." But Kenneth and Rita Coosewoon explained that this definition of Coosewoon is not correct. According to Rita Coosewoon, who is an acknowledged expert of the Comanche

On April 11, 2015, Kenneth Coosewoon sat in his favorite chair at his mother's home in Meers, Oklahoma. While visiting that day, Kenneth explained that he looked a great deal like Old Man Titchywhy, his Comanche grandfather who had five wives, all sisters but one, including his grandmother Coosewoon, from whom his family took their name. When Titchywhy moved to the reservation, the agency forced him to take one wife. Coosewoon and her only child, Abner, left the family. Abner, Kenneth's father, took his mother's name, and thus began the family name of Coosewoon.

language today, the name has far deeper meaning than Gray Eyes. "It is hard to explain," Rita once said, "especially in the English language." They say the famous family name derives from Coosewoony, "which means something like looking through a cloud or fog, not being able to see very clearly." Rita Coosewoon, a foremost tribal linguist, explained this definition, saying the family name meant a condition making viewing and seeing difficult as if looking through a defused thick mist.

The word, Coosewoon, has deeper meaning especially for Kenneth Coosewoon. His name is symbolic of the early part of his life when he had a great deal of personal trouble finding his way and understanding his identity as a Native American in the twentieth century. During the early part of his life, Kenneth Coosewoon struggled to find his correct direction and passionate path in life. During his early life, Kenneth Coosewoon often walked through a thick fog, often not knowing the best road for him to travel. As a result, Kenneth often wandered down the wrong roads, taking destructive paths that nearly killed him.

Coosewoon grew into a strong, attractive, and energetic athlete when he was a young man, earning a basketball scholarship to college. In high school, Kenneth met Doraline Taylor and later married her. Doraline was Kenneth's first wife, and after her death, he married Rita Barnhardt. At the same time that the couple married, Kenneth started drinking alcohol, which became a dangerous habit that he found hard to break. After a short stint in the United States Army, where Coosewoon injured his right shoulder, he received an honorable discharge. He and Doraline returned to the area around Lawton, Oklahoma, where they continued their life together, ultimately adding two children to their family. From his college days forward, Kenneth had a difficult time with alcohol, and became an alcoholic.

His journey in life proved unbearable at times for Kenneth and his extended family, and during his darkest days, Coosewoon attempted suicide. He failed at his attempts to kill himself, and every time he tried, he found that life continued and he had to adapt. Kenneth Coosewoon struggled to cope with everyday life and drank to excess until Doraline called an ambulance to take Kenneth to the Indian hospital in Lawton.

During Coosewoon's stay in the hospital, he experienced several spiritual events that changed his life forever. He stopped drinking on January 9, 1974, and each year he celebrates his second birthday—his sobriety birthday. Kenneth's life started anew in 1974 as he began walking the "Good Red Road." Kenneth joined an American Indian group of Alcoholics Anonymous, beginning his journey down the Red Road of health, happiness, and sobriety. He has never turned back to the old life and he began living for others in the light of the Spirit. Richard Downey of the Indian Health Service helped Kenneth begin a career in the field of drug and alcohol treatment. "With the help of Mr. Downey, I began work as a director of the treatment center" designed to help American Indian drug and alcohol users end their addictions.

While working as director of a treatment program situated at the old Fort Sill Indian School in Lawton, Kenneth attended a workshop for directors at Dwight Mission located in the heart of Cherokee Country. Coosewoon attended the second Sweat Lodge Ceremony of his life in the woods behind Dwight Mission. He camped with other men along Sallisaw

Kenneth had a close relationship with his mother, Mattie Kauley Coosewoon. They disagreed on matters of religion, but his mother was deeply influential in Kenneth's life. She was a renowned Kiowa beader and had deep knowledge of Kiowa and Comanche history. She lived to see him begin his journey as a spiritual man who dedicated his life to helping others.

Creek and attended a ceremony conducted by Lakota healer and Medicine Man Wallace Black Elk. Gracie Black Elk assisted her husband, and she knew Kenneth was a healer, well before Kenneth received his vision and would understand this role for himself. Knowing Kenneth's power, Gracie gave him the Calling and Healing songs of her Lakota people. Wallace and Gracie Black Elk's life-long relationship with Kenneth led him to understand his path as a healer and the importance of the Sweat Lodge Ceremony.

During a Sweat Lodge Ceremony, Kenneth experienced the Great Vision of his life, a revelation that changed his life from that day forward. The Grandfather asked Kenneth to lead the Sweat Lodge Ceremony and heal people. During the vision, Coosewoon received the Blue Medicine, which became part of his medicine ways. When Kenneth returned home from his adventure on Sallisaw Creek, he faced his first challenge as a healer. He helped save the life of his daughter's boyfriend who was shot and went through a harrowing experience. His injury led Kenneth to lead a series of Sweat Lodge Ceremonies with his clients on Cache Creek near the old Fort Sill Indian boarding school. Saving the life of this young man led Kenneth into his new life as a healer. Through his spiritual experiences and personal revitalization, Kenneth learned through the Grandfather and his experiences that his life was about helping to heal people.

Before a Sweat Lodge Ceremony, Kenneth prays to Grandfather asking for guidance in helping others. He holds sweetgrass and sage in his hand, sacred plants that send prayers to Grandfather. The creation of a Sweat Lodge includes the placement of a staff near the lodge. In this photograph, the staff holds an eagle feather and gourd dipper. Notice Kenneth's drum and beater as well as his cedar medicine box.

With time and patience, Kenneth learned to heal through the Spirit and the application of spiritual medicine, prayers, and Sweat Lodge Ceremonies. After his first healing Ceremonies, Kenneth continued to perform Sweat Lodge Ceremonies to help himself and others. Since that time, he has helped hundreds of people. Between 1978 and 2015, Kenneth entered many prisons in Oklahoma and beyond the state, and he lent his healing touch to many returning combat veterans and small children that had been traumatized. The accounts unfolded here offer a few samples of his healing Ceremonies and prayer encounters that brought about healing. The examples provided in this account are but a few of the many healings Coosewoon experienced while helping other people.

Examples of Coosewoon's healing used in this work illustrate a form of indigenous healing, most often through the Sweat Lodge Ceremony but Kenneth also uses prayer and ritual outside the Sweat Lodge to effectuate healings. All of the authors have witnessed Kenneth's healing ways and his forms of spiritual healing. Using Sweat Lodge and spiritual healing, Kenneth Coosewoon has helped numerous unnamed people. He has touched the lives of thousands of people during the last part of the late twentieth and early twenty-first centuries. He continues to use his healing power to help others and provide lectures to students of the American Indian and religious studies about his personal path on the Good Red Road. Following his Great Vision, the gift of Blue Medicine, and his use of the Sweat Lodge Ceremony, Kenneth Coosewoon has walked in the light of Grandfather. He has fulfilled the wishes of the Grandfather who asked Kenneth to help others and lead the Sweat Lodge Ceremony. His life is a testimony to Native American medicine ways, a life well lived with meaning and gifting of Grandfather's blessings.

Kenneth Coosewoon found what was missing in his life when he learned to lead the Sweat Lodge. In this illustration, Kenneth has framed the ribs of a Sweat Lodge in preparation of a ceremony. Note the shovel nearby in preparation of digging the rock pit. According to Kenneth, the pit may be dug first or after the frame is completed.

Chapter I

Coosewoon's Journey Through The Fog

By Clifford E. Trafzer

American Indians hold a special place in the nation's history. Diverse indigenous populations of North, South, and Central America enjoyed unique cultures and colorful histories long before the arrival of newcomers from foreign lands. Native Americans have always practiced various forms of religion and spiritual traditions, most often led by men and women recognized for their particular powers and gifts to heal, predict the weather, find game animals, determine when to plant, find lost items, and counsel those in need of guidance. All of the tribes and bands found within the Native Universe had specific names for their healers, birthing doctors, dentists, wound and bone physicians, chemists, pharmacists, and many others.

However, in the English language, non-Indians have often used the general terms of medicine men or medicine women to describe Native American healers. These individuals generally attributed their power to heal as a gift from the spirit world, another plain of being that influences life on earth. As a result of their gift to heal, most tribal members hold these special individuals in high esteem and some fear medicine people, since the healers had power to do both positive and negative actions toward other people. Healers hold dynamic space within tribal histories and are known best by their communities. This remains the case today, as many indigenous communities throughout the Native Universe honor their healers.

Over the years, I have interviewed Native American healers, spiritual leaders, and people of power living within contemporary indigenous communities. For the past seven years, Comanche healer Kenneth Coosewoon agreed to meet with me and allow me to interview him about his life as a healer. The following narrative is a condensed version of many of the stories Coosewoon shared through a series of oral interviews that I recorded on DVDs and in holograph in my journal from 2008 to 2015.

Coosewoon's story, especially about attaining his power and using it to heal others, is as compelling as any shared in the historical and anthropological literature. Once Kenneth experienced his Great Vision and received his Blue Medicine, he spent his life helping others. He has never received money for healing or conducting ceremony for others, but he has been rewarded many fold by the deep respect and appreciation given him by the thousands of people he has helped in the past. My association with Kenneth Coosewoon began when Cherokee nurse and healer Beverly Sourjohn Patchell invited me to visit Oklahoma to meet some of the indigenous healers that had influenced her life.

Flying Over an Indigenous Landscape

In April 2008, I flew from Ontario, California, to Oklahoma City. Not long after taking off, we flew over the Santa Rosa Mountains, Palm Springs, California, and along the northern-most edge of the Salton Sea. Not far to the east, we flew over the Colorado River near Blythe, California, where I could clearly make out the great and distinctive mountain, Picacho, a sacred peak to Yuman people located in Southern

California along the Colorado River near Horseshoe Bend. Picacho is a holy monument to the Quechan of Fort Yuma and other indigenous people of Arizona and California. I grew up in Yuma, Arizona, and have known Picacho since I was ten. As a boy, I visited Picacho with Mike Mendival, a man born in 1900 at Picacho Landing. From my seat on the south side of the airplane, I could easily see Picacho and marvel at the snaking river that flowed south from Blythe, past Picacho, on its way to El Gulfo in Mexico.

    As we flew over the Colorado River into Arizona, I saw the ancient indigenous trail that ran from the river southeast of Blythe to the Kofa and Castle Dome mountains into the desert east of the Colorado River. I could see portions of the trail that led across the Colorado Desert to the Gila River and east toward the home of Pima and Maricopa people, not far from present-day Phoenix. Farther east, we passed over the south rim of the Grand Canyon, before gliding effortlessly through the blue sky over New Mexico, the home of many Pueblo people, Jicarilla Apache, and Navajo. Before reaching the Panhandle of Texas and entering airspace over Oklahoma, I had a great deal of time to think about meeting Kenneth Coosewoon, the renown and notable Native American healer. This would be the first of many meetings and the beginning of a research project that continues today.

Meeting the Coosewoons and Healing Powers

    Before arriving in Oklahoma in April, I had previously met Rita Coosewoon, the second wife of Kenneth. For many years, Rita had participated with Kenneth in healing ceremonies, usually Sweat Lodge Ceremonies, and she had played an integral part in the ceremony as the female complement to Kenneth's male energy. As I would later learn, Kenneth believed the healing power "came in much stronger when both men and women are involved." I had enjoyed my first meeting with Rita at the University of Oklahoma where Beverly Patchell had organized a dynamic conference on American Indian medicine. After meeting Rita, I invited Beverly and Rita to participate in a consultation about American Indian medicine at the Smithsonian's National Museum of the American Indian in Washington, D. C.

As I flew into Will Rogers Airport in Oklahoma City, I considered past events I had experienced with these two engaging women, and my thoughts returned to the early 1970s when I was a Ph. D. student at Oklahoma State University. I looked forward in anticipation to meeting Kenneth Coosewoon and reconnecting with Beverly and Rita.

For many years, I had studied American Indian medicine, spiritual power, medicine people, and their

For special events, Kenneth Coosewoon wears his hair in braids and sports his ribbon shirts. In this photograph, Kenneth wears a bone choker and presents a stunning figure of a Comanche man that follows the Good Red Road.

influences within indigenous communities and beyond. Historically, American Indian healers such as Kenneth Coosewoon had played a significant role in the cultures of indigenous people, in the Americas as well as within the indigenous communities around the world. Healers are a special group of human beings. Many Native Americans believe they have the ability to harness the power of the "healing spirit" and use their gifts to help others by directing healing energy into patients via prayer, song, ritual, and material items such as medicine bundles. Most healers use their talents to heal people, and they use their gifts to save lives, advise patients, counsel about disease prevention and causation, and work with patients to get well. Most medicine men and women explain that the Creator gave them the gift of healing, which separates them from medical doctors trained in the schools of medicine within the Western World.

Medical doctors do not necessarily have the spiritual gift of healing. They attain their healing knowledge of Western medicine through formal education at schools of medicine, which generally have little or no relationship to spiritual gifts of healing (although some medical doctors believe in the healing spirit and sometimes pray with and for patients). Native American doctors often report that they received their charge to heal others from the Creator or creative forces—healing spirits identified by Kenneth Coosewoon as "the Grandfather." According to many traditional healers, including Kenneth, the Grandfather or Creator selected them to help other people. In a Native sense of understanding, the ability to heal others is a gift of the Spirit. This is certainly the case with Kenneth Coosewoon, who says that the Grandfather gave him the ability to heal people through the Great Vision. Indian doctors might learn elements of ceremony, ritual, songs, medical techniques, and medicinal knowledge from other Indian doctors, family experts in herbal medicine, and tribal elders. However, for many indigenous medicine people, the power to heal emerges from a spiritual, otherworldly sphere.

Listening and Learning from the Grandfather

Through the spirit world, an indigenous person—such as Kenneth Coosewoon—might learn about their calling to help others. They often learned their special methods of healing others. Through spiritual visitations, a potential Native American doctor might learn healing or calling songs. They often learned the power of their personal familiar, which might be a bird, animal, cloud, water, wood, or other element of nature that visits the doctor and helped him or her deliver the power that can be directed by the medicine man or woman into the ill person. In addition, a potential Indian doctor might learn new dances, rituals, or ceremonies given by the Creator or creative forces from the spirit world. In these ways, medicine people might learn their place within the community and world as well as ways they can help others. Some Indian doctors say they dream their healing power, while others point out that spiritual, creative, and healing forces visited them at night or during the day to impart power and knowledge to heal. At times, spiritual forces might visit potential Native healers through visions, dreams, or natural phenomena. At times, the Creator delivers healing power during meteor showers, earthquakes, or prolonged illnesses. During these special times, spiritual beings or creators may endow power to medicine men and women, enabling them to help and heal patients.

According to Kenneth Coosewoon, the Creator visited him directly, although at the time of his direct spiritual events, Kenneth did not recognize the voice or vision he saw as the Grandfather. In retrospect, he believes the Grandfather visited and spoke to him. Since the Great Vision, Coosewoon reported he had heard the voice of the Creator many times, fulfilling a promise made during the Great Vision, "I will always be with you. Whatever you need, I will provide." The Great Spirit commissioned Coosewoon to lead the Sweat Lodge Ceremony in order to heal others, and has often received advice when he was in prayer asking for assistance.

While I had met other Native American healers in past years, Beverly Patchell assured me that Coosewoon would prove to be a very unique person, a wonderful teacher, and a willing partner in sharing detailed and sensitive knowledge. Beverly was correct. From the first day I met Kenneth Coosewoon until the present, he has been a model consultant. He has been consistently frank, offering detailed information that has informed this work. Coosewoon has been completely open, forthright, and truthful about the things he knew first hand and he was never shy about providing information and details, many of which were unflattering to Kenneth. Since the days of his Great Vision, Kenneth has been transparent in about his life and healing, centering his life on helping others and following the Good Red Road of sobriety.

Visiting Cherokee Country and Healers

After landing at Will Rogers Airport, I checked out my rental car and met Beverly. Within a short time, we were driving east across the central plains of Oklahoma on a gray turnpike, watching patches of barren woods pass by. In our white car, we traveled east toward Tulsa, talking endlessly about families, friends, activities, and medicine ways. We stopped once to pay our toll at the turnpike gate, but other than that, we traveled pell-mell toward the Cherokee capital of Tahlequah, Oklahoma. We reached Tahlequah, Beverly's birthplace, before traveling on to Keys, Oklahoma, where we each took a room at a log motel. Keys, Oklahoma is located only a few miles from the Cherokee capital and home of many Native Americans. Beverly told me that for a few years, Kenneth Coosewoon had worked at Tahlequah, helping Cherokee children and healing anyone that asked for help. The wooded and hilly area around Tahlequah offered a landscape quite different from Kenneth's home on the Southern Plains of southwestern Oklahoma. But the woods and lakes provided an inviting environment and magical space in the hills of eastern Oklahoma. Keys provided a pleasant base for us as we traveled in many directions in the region, returning to Keys to record our travels and experiences. However, Tahlequah served as the center of our visit to Cherokee Country. Tahlequah is situated in a small urban center and home of Northeastern Oklahoma State University.

Tahlequah is much different from Oklahoma City or Lawton, Oklahoma. The Cookson Hills of eastern Oklahoma offer beautiful forests, rounded hills, jagged mountains, and grassy valleys with a good deal of water and rainfall. When we arrived in April, most trees had no leaves, but the redbud trees had started to show their brilliant deep red color and innate natural beauty. The serene scenery of Oklahoma surrounded us, enveloping us as we traveled the rural routes of the region. We could see several red bud trees in the thick woods of Cherokee Country, and we shared our admiration of these delightful creations. The first full day in the Cherokee Country, we traveled through the hills to meet a few medicine men. These men had been Beverly's mentors, teaching her some of the medicine ways of her people. We traveled past Ten Killer Lake and south into the Cookson Hills, following unpaved rural roads to the Stokes Stomp Grounds.

The Stomp Grounds is near the historic log-hewn home of Red Bird Smith, who fought for Cherokee sovereignty in the face of the United States and its policies of land allotment. In the nineteenth century, Red Bird had led a minor rebellion against the Dawes Severalty Act and started the Nighthawk Keetoowah Society among Cherokee traditionalists. Today, Red Bird's direct descendent, Crosslin Smith, lives on the property once inhabited by the famous Cherokee leader. Like most other indigenous healers, creative and spiritual forces charged Smith to be an Indian doctor, and heal others. The power had come to him in a special manner. For many years, Crosslin has practiced his medicine ways within the log cabin of Red Bird Smith. Over the years, although the Smith family had added onto the cabin, Crosslin kept the structure much as it had been in the nineteenth century and met patients in the old log structure. We visited Crosslin in this portion of the house, enjoying the warmth of the space and beauty of the cut timbers.

Wisdom of Crosslin Smith and Lessons From Stokes Stomp Grounds

While we were at Stokes, we listened and learned from Smith, a man of wisdom and strength. In his deep, commanding voice, Crosslin spoke at length about how he had received his healing power and used it to help people. Cherokee elder and healer Smith shared several stories with us and offered the following words about the healing spirit that mirrors the philosophy of Kenneth Coosewoon, the famed Comanche healer.

We got so much to learn
Spirit and how it works
Healing comes from Creator
Everyone is extended the gift of Spirit
Extended concepts of spirituality
Extended an invisible Spirit
Not an object born of you
Spirit within
He gave Spirit to everything
Connected Spirit with plants
Spirit of self
Spirit radiates Spirit.

We spent over an hour with Crosslin before a few patients knocked on his door and asked for his assistance. That was our signal to leave, and Beverly drove slowly from Crosslin's log dwelling to the Stokes Stomp Grounds where we stopped for a short visit at the sacred space. We remained at the Stomp Grounds a short while, paying homage and respect to the ancient dances the Cherokee had brought with them from the Southeast. Like the Choctaw, Chickasaw, Seminole, and Muscogee-Creek, the United States had forced the Cherokee and many other Eastern Woodland Indians into the Indian Territory. State and federal governments stole the lands of the Eastern Indian Nations, but the governments and settlers could not take the Spirit from the tribal people. Stokes Stomp Grounds represents the survival of the Cherokee Spirit that played a major role in the cultural continuance of the people. We spent a little time admiring the Stokes Stomp Grounds and its seven distinct arbors. Signs posted all around the stomp grounds asked visitors not to take pictures, so we honored the request and simply sat a spell and looked on at the ceremonial site where Cherokees and their neighbors gathered to do Stomp Dances.

The Cherokee share the Stomp Dance tradition with several other tribes from the Eastern Woodlands, and the ceremony is connected to the Green Corn Ceremony in which dancers and singers shuffle and stomp in a circle close to the Mother Fire, a sacred and living element of the Stomp Dance. The ceremony lasts from dusk to dawn, and pledges agree to participate in the all-night ceremony. Men and women participate in the ceremony, and men wear traditional rattles made from the shells of box turtles. Outside the inner earthen circle, representatives of the seven clans occupy their arbors.

While surveying the Stomp Grounds, Crosslin's words spun around in my head. I kept thinking about their meaning and the role the healing spirit has played throughout Native American history. Spirit medicine was on my mind as Beverly and I drove slowly over the gravel, dirt, and paved roads through the woods. We zigzagged through the countryside until I became totally lost. To me, the unimproved roads seemed like a confusing, endless maze. Fortunately, Beverly drove us through the woods and hills until we reached pavement. Otherwise, I would have been lost.

Watt Cheater and Jim Henson

Beverly drove through the winding roads of the Cookson Hills on our way to the home of Watt Cheater, another Cherokee medicine man who lived in Marble City, Oklahoma. Watt was in his 90s, approximately 96 or 97, and the week before our visit, he had experienced a stroke. Still, he greeted us with a big smile and measured laughter.

He was glad to see "Nurse Woman" and meet me. He made us welcome. Before we arrived, Beverly had bought Watt a warm lunch, which he ate with gusto and sincere appreciation. While we talked, Watt doctored himself with homemade herbal medicines that he had set on his coffee table. He put his medicine on his legs and chest. Like other "medicine men," especially Kenneth Coosewoon, Watt refused to consider himself a medicine man. He simply said, "I help people, that's what I do." Coosewoon is of the same mind. He is not comfortable with the label of medicine man but recognizes that he is a healer because of the spiritual gift given him. "I've done every rotten thing you can think of and if the Grandfather can forgive me and ask me to help others, then anyone can help others."

Watt was most hospitable and spoke freely about his work helping others and playing professional baseball in California "back in the day." Beverly and I remained at Watt's house in Marble City only a short time because of Watt's ill health and his tired state. So we left Marble City and Watt's house, traveling on our way back to Keys. Along the way, Beverly told me about Dwight Mission, a Baptist Mission and Indian school located in Vian, Oklahoma. Dwight Mission had been the site of Christian education for Indian children, and the institution had educated many Cherokee children over several years.

Dwight Mission had been a boarding school for children, and like all the Indian boarding schools, the school grounds included a cemetery where teachers, ministers, and students had buried students that died while attending the school. As we approached Dwight Mission, we could see the large, red-colored mission nestled neatly on a hill not far from a heavily wooded area.

Today, the Dwight Mission serves as a conference center, and when Beverly drove past the mission, we saw that people engaged the mission for an event. Rather than drive up to the old church, Beverly turned onto the road leading into the cemetery. Dwight Mission had a fairly extensive cemetery. During the late nineteenth and early twentieth centuries, Indian boarding schools experienced the deaths of many children. When their families lived too far away, or when the child's parents belonged to the church, school officials and parents buried their children in the mission school cemetery. We paid our respects to the children buried at Dwight mission and walked down to the lower end of the cemetery. The mission sat on a hill to our right, back through the trees. To our left, a broad, open meadow appeared and a small stream snaked its way through the meadow and disappeared into the woods in front of us. We enjoyed the sunlight, songbirds, and rustling of the wind. Beverly began her description of the significant landscape in front of us. It is a holy and sacred site to Kenneth Coosewoon, the place where he had experienced his Great Vision and acquired his Blue Medicine.

"This is where Kenneth had his vision," Beverly explained. "He was camping down there with a group of directors working in the field of substance abuse. They held a Sweat Lodge Ceremony by the creek at the edge of the woods." She continued saying, "the men were conducting the Sweat Lodge Ceremony when Kenneth had a Great Vision and learned the Grandfather wanted him to run the Sweat Lodge and heal people." The site could not have been more beautiful. The season had turned toward spring, and life had started to unfold in the thick woods near Dwight Mission. Some trees in this area had buds and tiny leaves beginning to form. The air moved lightly, creating a clear, bright, and cheery day. The site was in the process of rebirth, just as Kenneth had been reborn in this special space located in the heart of Indian Country. At the lower end of the cemetery we studied the creek for a few minutes and watched the water ripple and move through the valley, disappearing below us into the woods. In front of us, beyond the fence line, appeared a spacious and inviting campground in the woods among the tall trees and near the small stream that sang as it rolled over the rocks and fallen logs. Beverly broke the silence saying, "it would be best for Kenneth to tell you what happened to him here because it changed his life forever." She mentioned again that the spiritual event that had happened here was so significant to Kenneth and to hundreds of people he had doctored over the years. She emphasized that it all began at Dwight Mission in the heart of the Cherokee Country—not his Native Comanche Country of southwestern Oklahoma.

After our visit to Dwight Mission, we drove back to Keys and our motel. That night, Beverly and I talked about our trip through the Cookson Hills before Jim Henson dropped by our rooms for a visit. Jim is a Cherokee healer who had once worked with Kenneth Coosewoon. The two healers knew each other. We spent three hours with Jim who generously shared his stories with us, telling us fascinating stories of his Grandfather's power and fight against an evil person that could shape shift. Without any hesitation, Jim explained in detail how his grandfather had given him the power to heal. Henson told many stories and invited us to his family's "old home place" where Jim had unearthed his grandfather's medicine bundle. Jim described how his grandfather had visited him in spirit and how the elder gave his old medicine bundle and healing power to Jim. We could have listened to Jim for hours, but it was late at night and he had not yet been home from his day's work. Jim ended our visit with a healing song and prayer for one of my friends battling breast cancer. He left and we rested a few hours before continuing our journey the next day.

Kenneth Coosewoon and
The American Medical Association

Early the next morning, we had breakfast in Tahlequah before heading south to visit a Cherokee artist that made dance outfits and turtle rattles. Then we headed southwest toward Oklahoma City. We made a brief stop to visit the Sac and Fox Reservation and see an area formerly struck by a meteor. The Sac and Fox also say Little People frequent the strike area. While visiting the heavy rocks located in a grove of trees, a man of power reported to me that my mother was present in spirit. He stated that my mother was glad that we were making this trip and studying the medicine ways of indigenous people. We continued our journey southwest to Oklahoma City where we participated in a meeting of the American Medical Association's Commission on Health Care Disparities (AMA). This was an honor and privilege for me, being an historian asked to address a group of medical doctors and health care providers interested in disparities.

On April 14, 2008, the night before the conference, I had dinner with Kenneth and Rita Coosewoon. We ate at the Cattlemen's Steak House near the Oklahoma City Stockyards. Kenneth and I had a chance to get to know each other, and I enjoyed our conversation. I found Kenneth to be a kind and open man, interested in many topics, including the medicine ways of diverse tribal people. He is a large built, powerful man with broad shoulders and strong physical strength. At the Cattleman's Steak House, Coosewoon shared some information about his Great Vision but few details. These things I would learn later. We were in a social setting and getting to know each other. He spoke only a little about his own experience of gaining power to heal, but he agreed to meet me the next day to share an oral history.

I visited with Rita Coosewoon and found her to be a generous and genuine tribal elder, a kind, intelligent, and soft-spoken woman with deep knowledge and a caring spirit. Rita is a strong Comanche woman and no man's fool. Underneath her natural beauty, she exhibited a strong personality and a will of steel, tempered by knowledge of Native American history, language, and culture. Today, she serves as a tribal judge for the Comanche Nation. As a small child, she had been placed in the Fort Sill Indian Boarding School in Lawton, Oklahoma, an off-reservation federal Indian boarding school where she suffered emotional stress. Yet, in spite of mean spirited ridicule and severe corporal and verbal punishment at school, Rita turned the power and used her boarding school days to advance herself, her family, and her people.

Rita tenaciously held onto her language, a treasure that she refused to surrender. As a result of her language abilities, experts today recognize Rita as one of the foremost (if not the foremost) experts of the Comanche language. For many years, she taught the Comanche language to people of all ages and in many different venues. She has taught Comanche in schools and community colleges and participates in the international language association devoted to preserving Uto-Aztecan languages.

Previous to our dinner at the steak house, I had met Rita Coosewoon at another event sponsored by Beverly Patchell and the University of Oklahoma. In 2005 I attended a national conference sponsored by the Native American Native Alaskan Nurses Association at the University of Oklahoma College of Nursing. This conference focused on Native American healing, and our mutual friend Beverly coordinated the event. I learned of the event from Lumbee elder Helen Scheirbeck, an administrator at the National Museum of the American Indian. I had met Rita at the conference held on the main campus of the University of Oklahoma, at the Health Sciences Center. At the same conference where I met Rita, I also met Beverly, a dynamic and down to earth scholar and professor. She is also a Native healer in her own right, and I enjoyed meeting both women. Helen told me about Beverly and reported that she had helped her and others through her Native medicine ways. Helen had the highest regards for Beverly as a health care provider and as a traditional healer. She urged me to attend the conference, which led to meeting many marvelous educators and traditional healers, including Kenneth Coosewoon. Beverly was, and remains, a leader of Indian health among indigenous people.

At the time of the first conference at the University of Oklahoma in 2005, Kenneth was ill and unable to attend. But I had an opportunity to get to know Beverly and Rita. Meeting them also led to working with both of them on an exhibit project sponsored by the National Institutes of Health (NIH) and the National Library of Medicine (NLM). During the first conference, Rita and Beverly ran a Sweat Lodge

Ceremony on campus. Rita's son, Sheldon, tended the fire and brought hot rocks into the Sweat Lodge for participants. Through Beverly and Rita, I came to learn more about Kenneth and grew in my admiration of this unusual man. However, I did not meet him until April 2008 at the gathering in Oklahoma City to discuss health care disparities among Native Americans, past and present.

The morning following our dinner at the Cattlemen's Steak House in 2008, I met Kenneth and Rita at the University of Oklahoma Medical Center in Oklahoma City. To open the conference in a good way, Kenneth and Rita Coosewoon gave the opening invocation with songs and prayers. They provided a ceremonial welcome through song and story. I attended the meeting of the American Medical Association's Commission meeting with great anticipation. I had long wanted to meet Kenneth Coosewoon and reconnect with Rita and Beverly. Kenneth wore a red ribbon shirt, and he spoke with great authority about the importance of our meeting. When Kenneth and Rita finished, Beverly arranged for me to conduct an oral interview.

When the conference opened, I gave the first presentation on historical health care disparities among selected Native Americans. Using historical statistics I had gathered through death certificates among the Confederated Yakama Tribe and death registers of the 29 tribes of the Mission Indian Agency of Southern California, I painted a detailed comparative picture of deaths caused by infectious disease among these Native Americans during the early twentieth century. I provided crude death rates resulting from tuberculosis, pneumonia, influenza, measles, gastro-intestinal diseases, and other diseases, comparing death rates and other statistics among Native Americans with those of the general population of the United States, white Americans, and African Americans.

Kenneth's Kiowa cousin, Dr. Everett Rhoades, and his daughter also presented on health care disparities but those of more recent years. For many years Dr. Rhoades had served as the head of the Indian Health Service, and both he and his daughter, also a medical doctor, gave revealing lectures on Native American health disparities. All of the talks proved informative and engaging. However, nothing compared with my opportunity to meet with and come to know Kenneth and Rita Coosewoon over dinner and in my hotel room. There, I conducted my first of many oral histories with Kenneth Coosewoon. Most of what is known about the life and work of Coosewoon emerged from these oral interviews, given to me with permission from 2008 to 2015.

Interviewing Kenneth Coosewoon

Given my past research and publishing about Native American medicine ways, I remember treasuring my meeting with Kenneth and Rita Coosewoon as well as the opportunity to present some of my research on health care disparities to members of the American Medical Association. I hoped that my presentation and those of others would encourage funding sources, including federal dollars and private foundations, to pay greater attention to American Indian health and provide resources and pressure to fund Indian health initiatives. However, I was also extremely interested in learning details of Kenneth's healing experiences and more about his Great Vision. At the time, I knew only sketches of his Great Vision that he had experienced thirty or more years before. I fully understood that his vision had taken

This is a candid picture of Kenneth's mother-in-law, Aline Taylor. Her loved ones called her Memo. She was Doraline's mother, and at first, she opposed her daughter's marriage to Kenneth. But over the years she formed a strong and lasting relationship with Kenneth and her granddaughters.

Coosewoon on a new path that led to his life's work as a traditional Indian healer. Of course the Great Vision was a significant and life-changing event for Kenneth Coosewoon, but initially, he did not discuss his Great Vision in any detail. Perhaps he wanted to know more about me personally and my scholarly work before delving deeply into his personal and spiritual life. He likely wanted to know how I might use his story and whether or not I would present his history in an accurate and sensitive manner, especially since a great deal of the story focused on the Spirit or Grandfather, as Kenneth referred to the Creator, God, Almighty, or what others may call the Supreme Being or Master of Life. Much of what we know of Kenneth's revelations stem from his memory and oral histories, although Rita Coosewoon, Beverly Patchell, and Ronald Cooper have also contributed to this knowledge of past events.

Over time, Coosewoon shared more and more of his personal stories. His life history unfolded over time and ever so slowly. Each time we met, I learned something new and additional details to stories he had told me before. Without fail, each time we met he added significant new information. The interviews created a methodological process that developed naturally and in good measure over time.

Kenneth gave his stories willingly each time we conducted an interview. Gradually, Kenneth unfolded his life's history, providing both positive and negative aspects of his life. For Kenneth, and many Native American elders I have known, to tell too much of their life's story too quickly would constitute bragging. Kenneth was far too humble to brag about his abilities and his healing experiences. He was always self-effacing.

My notes from our conservation at the Cattleman's restaurant are sketchy, as we were in conversation, and I had little time to record in my Journal. Later that evening, but not at the Cattleman's Steak House, I wrote regarding Kenneth's Great Vision at Dwight Mission. On the evening of April 14, 2008, I wrote: "While tending the Sweat Lodge fire by himself, a blue chip came from the fire. He picked it up and was drawn to the creek where a great storm emerged close to him with thunder and lightning. A great wind, roaring like a train, came down the creek, the breath of the Spirit. Then the ground trembled and trees bent over, while dancing. Creator Grandfather spoke to Kenneth, telling him to do the Sweat Lodge Ceremony, to bring it back to life."

This note in my Journal initiated my research with Kenneth, investigating and interpreting Kenneth's life work as a traditional Native American medicine man. Since 2008, I have met with Kenneth and Rita many times, especially when they traveled to Southern California to lecture at the University of California, Riverside. Over the years, I have conducted several oral interviews with the Coosewoons, and each time we completed an oral history, I learned more. We often coupled our oral history sessions with other activities in Southern California, which brought the Coosewoons, Beverly Patchell, and Ronald Cooper (Kenneth's grandson) to the region where we could work. For example, we did an oral history in April 2012 when the Coosewoons and Beverly Patchell traveled to Southern California. At that time, Beverly, Rita, and Kenneth provided a lecture on healing through the Sweat Lodge as part of our annual Medicine Ways Conference at the University of California, Riverside.

During the same week, Ronald Cooper gave a separate lecture about his hike on the Trail of Tears and the book he produced on his experiences. Cooper also joined in a lengthy lecture on Sweat Lodge in the Highlander Union Building. While this group from Oklahoma visited the area to lecture, we conducted one of several oral interviews and discussed how we would coordinate the writing of this work. Whenever we were together our conversations invariably circled back to Kenneth and his work as a healer. Since 1978, Kenneth has doctored thousands of people and conducted thousands of Sweat Lodge Ceremonies, helping anyone and everyone that asked for aid. This has been his life for over thirty years, and during his visits to the Medicine Ways Conference, he met with people to conduct short healing and prayer ceremonies, helping people with cancer, heart disease, alcoholism, and spinal injuries. For his help on these occasions, Kenneth asked no payment of money as he always shares his gift freely with anyone that asks. He has healed people of cancer, cirrhosis, heart ailments, and depression. He has healed people successfully but not everyone. He explains he has no control over who gets healed. He explains that the Grandfather decides and brings the healing. Coosewoon is simply a conduit of that healing power.

During the Medicine Ways Conference at the University of California, Riverside, Coosewoon did not perform complete Sweat Lodge Ceremonies. But in the past, he has performed ceremony at many locations throughout the United States, taking people into the Sweat Lodge to pray and sing, asking the Grandfather to provide the healing needed by each person in attendance. He has conducted Sweat Lodge Ceremonies at several conferences and multiple prisons. He has also helped military veterans recover from the physical, mental, and spiritual ill effects of war. He has even helped cleanse a group of devil worshippers, so they could leave evil behind and seek the blessings of the Grandfather. He has offered his healing ways generously and unselfishly.

In 1978, Kenneth began his healing path, using his gift to benefit others. However, his life did not start out that way. Kenneth was not born into the healing tradition of the Sweat Lodge. Indeed, as a young man and into early adulthood, he did not follow the Good Red Road. He lived life on the edge, a dangerous life as an alcoholic. Kenneth learned what it meant to be without hope of ever living a normal life. Feelings of hopelessness would help him in the future as director of drug and alcohol centers for American Indians and as a medicine man. Kenneth spent the first part of his life

Over the years, Kenneth built many Sweat Lodges, far too many to count. He conducted many ceremonies in lodges that looked much like the one in this photograph. It is representative of the kind of lodge built by many Plains Indians and other indigenous people across the Western Hemisphere.

trying to find his identity as a Native American living in the middle of the twentieth century while fighting an addiction to drugs and alcohol. In many ways, Kenneth's early life matched his family name, Coosewoon, which Rita once explained, "means like going through a cloud or fog, trying to see." Coosewoon spent his early life trying to understand the meaning of his life with many dark clouds in his path. But these clouds and fogs lifted after his Great Vision, giving him a purpose in life based on helping others. Like the heroes found in the ancient Native American narratives, Coosewoon began living life for the benefit of others, not his own pleasure or gratification. His vision set him on the Good Red Road that he has walked since the 1970s.

Early Life: Among Comanche and Kiowa

Kenneth Ray Coosewoon was born on September 29, 1929 in the heart of Comanche and Kiowa Country. He grew up near Medicine Park, Oklahoma, in the shadow of Mount Scott, a sacred mountain to many Native Americans. Coosewoon was born into a mixed Native family: his father was Comanche and his mother was Kiowa, descendants of superior warrior families. Kenneth spent the early years of his life in Comanche County, Oklahoma. He grew up on his mother's home place in Meers, Oklahoma near Medicine Park, where he still lives. Coosewoon spent his life on the land settled by his mother's family. After marrying Mattie Kauley, Kenneth's father, Abner Coosewoon, took up residence in the old home place of the Kauley family. In accordance with the laws of the United States, children of American Indians, including children of mixed Indian blood, can be enrolled only in one tribe. Abner enrolled Kenneth as a member of the Comanche Nation of Oklahoma, and he has lived his life honoring his Comanche blood while never forgetting his mother's Kiowa people.

Today, Kenneth has relatives among the Kiowa and Comanche people, and he is proud of both sides of his family. He is especially proud of Dr. Everett Rhoades, the former Director of the Indian Health Service, and his children. Kenneth's heritage as a Comanche and Kiowa directed his life's path, especially in mid-life when he learned more about the spiritual traditions of Plains Indians and the cultural significance of the Sweat Lodge Ceremony. Kenneth has spent most of his life dedicated to the preservation and use of living religious traditions of Indian people, sharing his knowledge and spirit with those in need of prayer and healing.

As a boy, Kenneth lived free on the endless rolling prairie of southwestern Oklahoma, a land blessed by the aged Mount Scott and the Wichita Mountains. The mountains, hills, and plains of the region also enjoy a few small creeks and rivers, some of which flow into Lake Lawtonka. Like other Indian families, the Coosewoons had horses, several horses among the immediate and extended family. Kenneth grew up on horseback, developing into a fine rider. All of the children he knew were adept with horses and they enjoyed riding the plains close to his home. He grew up around horses, learning to ride bareback as a small child. Some of his earliest memories revolve around horses and riding pell-mell over the Southern Plains.

During the 1930s, several Comanche and Kiowa families used horses and wagons as their principle means of transportation. They traveled into towns to buy flour, sugar, coffee, and other essentials. Money was scarce for most

Indian families of southwestern Oklahoma, and Kenneth learned to make do with little to eat and relish special foods and snacks that he received.

Like other Native American fathers and others living during the Great Depression, Abner Coosewoon hunted deer, rabbit, squirrel, prairie dog, and birds. Wild game supplemented the family diet, and at a young age, Kenneth learned to hunt and fish. Although he enjoyed fishing, he had more fun playing sports, especially football, basketball, baseball, boxing, and track and field.

He was a handsome and powerful young man. He was also a superior fighter that few people challenged. Kenneth became extremely popular at Elgin High School in Elgin, Oklahoma, where he excelled in basketball, earning state and county honors as a great athlete. Coosewoon made the all-state basketball team in the late 1940s, and after he graduated from high school in 1950, two colleges offered him athletic scholarships. While Kenneth was a young person, he focused his life on athletics and girls. During his youth, his mother became deeply involved in the Christian religion and became a leader in the local Kiowa Methodist Church. She continually

In his youth, Kenneth was a superior athlete. He was a star, all-state basketball player, but he also excelled in baseball, football, and boxing. He boxed professionally for a short time, and he used his skills as a boxer when he worked as a bouncer.

tried to draw Kenneth into the religion in a deep way, but he showed far more interest in athletics.

The Methodist Church, Athletics, and Alcohol

As a child, Kenneth's mother "got religion." She joined the Kiowa Methodist Church and encouraged her children to follow the Christian faith. Many Christian denominations, including Southern Methodists, encouraged Indians to give up traditional beliefs and ceremonies, including the Sweat Lodge. Many church leaders considered Native American beliefs to be backward, primitive, and savage. As a result, Kenneth grew up not knowing his mother's father had been the leader of the Sweat Lodge and had healed people. As a boy, Coosewoon tried to follow the teachings of the Methodist church and obey his parents and their Christian ways. His parents set outstanding examples as pious people. They never drank liquor. "My mother and dad," Kenneth explained, never took "a drink of any kind of alcohol." Later, Kenneth learned that his father never drank in front of the children, but he once admitted to Kenneth that "he got drunk one time in his life." Once was enough, so he quit drinking.

Kenneth took another path down a desperate trail that led him to excessive drinking and drugging. As a boy, he had attended Lake View School and Elgin High School with children from many diverse backgrounds, but most were Kiowa and Comanche children. Kenneth did fair in his academic work, but he excelled as a student athlete. "I was the most outstanding basketball player in Comanche County in 1949 and 1950." Weatherford College, known today as Southwestern Oklahoma State University at Weatherford, and Cameron College in Lawton, Oklahoma, offered Kenneth

Mount Scott Kiowa United Methodist Church was built in 1895. Kenneth's mother and relatives attended this church, and Kenneth attended services there many times. Kenneth lives within miles of the church situated in view of Lake Lawtonka and Mount Scott, a sacred mountain to many Native Americans.

basketball scholarships. He could have sought scholarships in football, baseball, track and field, and other sports, but Kenneth most enjoyed basketball, a very popular sport among many Native Americans. Kenneth chose to attend Cameron College where he became a star basketball player, boxer, and member of the track team. However, "somewhere down the line" he took his first drink of alcohol, which altered his life for many years.

"When I bought my first bottle of beer," Kenneth explained, "I liked what it done for me." In part, Coosewoon began drinking because of his situation as an Indian at a predominately white school—Cameron College. "I was an Indian among whites, going to a white school," Kenneth once explained, and he did not feel "quite as good" as non-Indian people, meaning he felt inferior. With a "few bottles of beer,"

Kenneth could transform himself into a real "Don Juan" and he "could whip anybody." Alcohol gave him false courage, and he set out to prove to others that he was faster, tougher, stronger, and better, even though he felt some inferiority while attending a white institution that admitted few Indian people.

These feelings extended to dating white girls attending college. "If you was a good Indian, they'd like you," Coosewoon stated, but pointed out, "but if you went with their daughter, they didn't want their daughter to go with you." Prejudice against American Indians has existed since the fifteenth century and was alive still during Coosewoon's youth just as it is today. This contradiction troubled Kenneth, who grew up wanting to believe that all people were equal, but college taught him that racism against Indians existed on and off reservations and in border towns near concentrations of Indians. In fact, Kenneth learned that racism existed everywhere. Racism was alive on college campuses in the mid-twentieth century!

In 1950, Kenneth chose to attend Cameron University in Lawton, Oklahoma, because of the basketball scholarship and its location close to his home in Medicine Park. Kenneth became very popular on the Cameron campus because of his athletic ability. He looked forward to playing basketball for the Cameron College Aggies. Kenneth had met the love of his young life, a dark-haired beauty named Doraline Taylor while attending Elgin High. Like Kenneth, Doraline attended Cameron College since the college was situated near her home at Lake Lawtonka.

Oklahoma educators established Cameron in 1909 and held the first class meetings of Cameron in the basement of a bank building. The school transformed from a high school to a community college, and eventually to a four-year college. It is a university today with approximately 6000 students, but when Coosewoon attended the school, it was a college with far fewer students. While at Cameron, Kenneth began to drink, to loosen up and be sociable with other students.   The handsome young man dated several women from many different backgrounds, but soon learned that although non-Indians appreciated his athletic prowess, they did not want him dating their non-Indian daughters. Even his relationship with Doraline was difficult from the start. Doraline was white and Kenneth was Indian. Neither set of parents wanted the couple to marry.

Before attending Cameron, Kenneth had limited experience dealing with non-Indians on a personal basis, but at college he learned about prejudice against Indian people. Kenneth and Doraline, however, connected on many levels and they were married on January 5, 1951. They honeymooned at the nicest place in downtown Lawton, Oklahoma—the Midland Hotel on 4th Street and C Avenue. At first neither set of parents liked the idea of the couple marrying, but with time they grew to like the match and accept the mixed racial marriage and their young in-laws. Many whites and Indians opposed mixed marriages, and several people voiced their opposition to the match. Their love developed in 1950 during the era of the Cold War in American history.

This was an era of anti-communism and developing civil rights for African Americans. But it was not a good time for Native Americans facing termination of Indian tribes by the federal government as well as relocation of young Native Americans into the cities of the United States. Still, the couple was devoted to each other, and they became closer to one another as time passed. At the time of their marriage, Kenneth was drinking but not in the excess that would develop later. Still, from the outset, Doraline had to adapt to Kenneth's drinking and the couple eventually encountered monumental personal problems, especially those associated with Kenneth's use of alchohol. Over time, they weathered these challenges together and grew closer. As Kenneth explained in simple terms, "this is because we loved each other."

Fighting, Drinking, and Marriage

While Kenneth attended high school and college, he developed a strong fighting spirit. Like Comanche warriors of former centuries, Kenneth became a dominant and threatening character on and off the athletic field. During his young adulthood, Coosewoon "was always trying to be a big shot or something." Kenneth showed no fear of anyone and "wouldn't let nobody know that I was scared of anybody or anything." Even if a challenger looked like he "was going to beat the heck out of me, I'd go out there and fight him anyway, just to show I wasn't scared." In retrospect, Coosewoon readily admits that such ideas were "crazy." Perhaps he used his fighting ability to overcome his insecurities of being an Indian, but whatever the reason, he would drink "a few beers then become the toughest man in Lawton." Today, he ponders whether or not he "was trying to be a man." In recent years, Kenneth suggested, "I was trying to prove I was a man." Kenneth followed the fighting trail for many years until spirits introduced him to a new way of thinking about who he was and the holy work he was to pursue for the benefit of others. In spite of his failures as a person, his one constant remained Doraline.

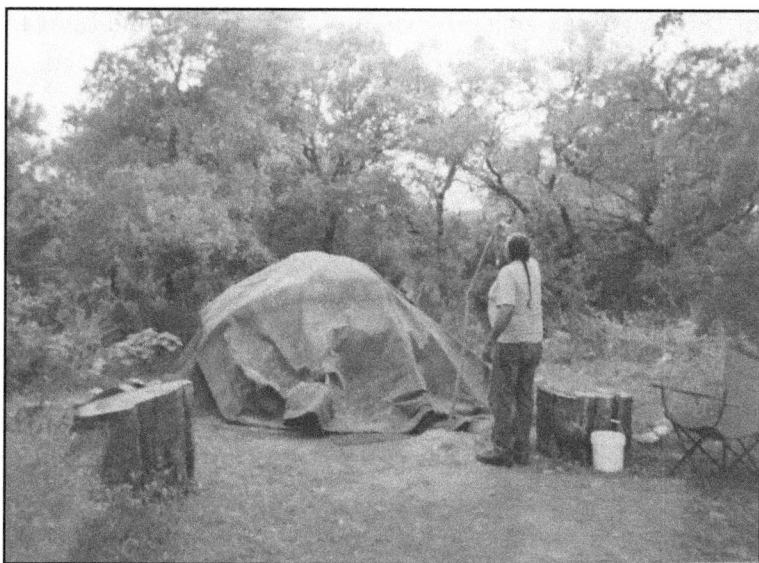

Kenneth is pictured here after completing the creation of a Sweat Lodge, including its canvas covering. Notice that Kenneth is hanging a medicine bundle that contains his Blue Medicine on the staff near the lodge. Kenneth and his family make medicine bags that they give to people in need of healing. Kenneth believes the bundles help ward off bad medicine that people can place on others to do them harm or make them ill.

With their 1951 marriage, the newlyweds decided to make their way through life together, agreeing to face all adversity and good—the great joys and multiple sorrows—as a team. Indian parents did not like their children marrying outsiders, especially white people whose ancestors had fought the Comanche and Kiowa during the Red River Wars. Comanche and Kiowa had lost their freedom, lands, and ways of life to white Americans and soldiers of the United States. Less than one hundred years before the Coosewoon's married, the Plains people had lost the millions of buffalo that had, for generations, fed, clothed, and provided tools for Comanche and Kiowa people. Coosewoon's family well knew that Americans had written the Medicine Lodge Treaty of 1867 that created a reservation for Comanche and Kiowa, and they had lived through the era when white Americans allotted reservation lands, divesting Native Americans of millions of acres of land.

Some Comanche lands proved rich in oil, water, range, and farmland. White Americans and their leaders had slaughtered nearly all the buffalo, and they had proclaimed that Indians were the "vanishing" Americans. Comanche and Kiowa men and women had survived, but they never forgot the injustices of past decades. Kenneth's mother and father had helped bring forth a new generation of indigenous people who had to cope with both worlds. This was the world of Kenneth and Doraline. Kenneth's parents had emerged from fighting warriors and supportive women that fought the United States Army and felt the sting of destructive Indian policies in the recent past. Initially, Kenneth's mother and father were very displeased their son had chosen to marry Doraline, but they learned to live with the decision and eventually found Doraline to be a fine and caring wife for their son. Many would consider her a saint for remaining loyal to Kenneth during difficult and trying times.

Joining the U.S. Army

After marrying Doraline, Kenneth joined the United States Army on January 29, 1951 and was mustered in at Fort Sill, Oklahoma. Put on a troop train, he was transported to Camp Atterbury, Indiana for his basic training. Watching Mount Scott slowly disappear in the train window brought a deeper sadness to Kenneth than he had known before. Kenneth and Doraline had decided to make the Army their career and looked forward to traveling and the security Army life would provide for them and their family. In addition, Kenneth wanted to fight for the United States, especially during the Korean War. Like many American Indians, past and present, Kenneth was very patriotic and wanted to use his warrior tradition to support the efforts of the United States overseas. Kenneth and Doraline dropped out of Cameron College and set out on their new adventure. At that time, Kenneth and Doraline had little or no money. The Army seemed like a serious career for the Coosewoons, and Kenneth followed the path of other Comanche people that had served in the armed forces during World War I, World War II, and the Korean War. The newlyweds saw the Army as an opportunity to further themselves and avoid the poverty at home.

For seven months and twenty days, Coosewoon served in the armed forces. Kenneth "wanted to go to Korea" and fight for the United States, but the Army stationed him at Fort Riley, Kansas, where he attended Officer Candidate School to qualify for the rank of a non-commissioned officer. He passed his leadership training and was made a sergeant. His unit was sent to Indiana and awaited orders to ship out to Germany. However, during a training exercise to learn how to use grenades, Kenneth severely dislocated his shoulder while throwing one. His shoulder dislocated badly, and had to be forced back into the socket. The injury proved very painful and life changing since it prevented him from shipping out with his unit. The Army never repaired Kenneth's arm and he has suffered severe pain from the injury ever since—with little help from the Veterans Administration to repair his shoulder dislocation. As a result of his injury, the Army placed him in a hospital where he received an honorable discharge because of his injury. His shoulder troubles him to this day. Kenneth served in the Army from January 29, 1951 to September 17, 1951. Following his medical release from the Army, he soon returned to Medicine Park with his young wife.

Self-Employment, Man Power Program, and Alcoholism

After returning to Medicine Park, Oklahoma, in the fall of 1951, Kenneth accepted a number of jobs including digging foundations for buildings at Fort Sill for $1 per hour. Doraline worked seven days a week for $17.50 per week. They lived in a one-bedroom apartment and shared a bathroom with two other couples. But, Kenneth also continued drinking, a habit that grew over time and began a path of destruction that lasted for years. Besides self-destruction, Coosewoon's drinking significantly affected his family, which suffered from his negative behavior. In part, his dependency on drugs and alcohol stemmed from an identity crisis surrounding Kenneth's life as a Native American living in the twentieth century, unlike previous centuries when Comanche and Kiowa people were totally independent from foreign rule and lived out their cultures in the ways of their grandparents, great-grandparents, and all the prior generations. Still, Kenneth was able to function sufficiently to receive a useful education.

In 1952 he attended a Technical Branch of Oklahoma A&M (now Oklahoma State University) in Okmulgee, Oklahoma, acquiring the trade of dry-cleaning. Kenneth learned his lessons well. He and Doraline worked for various dry cleaning shops over a period of ten years, first with Griswolds' in Lawton and later with Vernon Howell on the Fort Sill Army post. Kenneth excelled in his work. He worked for Vernon Howell until 1964 when the Coosewoons bought the business. From 1964 to 1975, Kenneth and Doraline Coosewoon owned and operated Ken's Cleaners in Lawton, Oklahoma, making a huge success of the business. But during all this time, Kenneth fell deeper into alcoholism, a disease that significantly impaired his judgment as well as his professional and personal life.

In 1975, Kenneth decided to leave Ken's Cleaners and end the everyday struggle to make a small business a success. Coosewoon began a new career of working for his tribe. Between 1974 and 1978, Kenneth worked as Assistant Director and Specialist for the Comanche Tribe Manpower Program, a project supported by the federal government as part of the Comprehensive Employment and Training Act (CETA). While working for the Manpower Project, Coosewoon supervised nine counselors and clerical assistants. He often interviewed prospective employers of Comanche people and helped develop job opportunities for tribal members. He worked closely with Comanche people to place them in meaningful positions. The project aimed at guiding Comanche into permanent positions and professions.

During the 1970s, Comanche County and the surrounding area constituted a depressed economic area, and Coosewoon worked diligently to find work for Indian people. In addition, he placed young people into jobs and vocational training programs while coordinating the Comanche Adult Education Program that channeled high school dropouts into GED programs. Over the years, he worked with over 1,200 people, making a contribution to the Comanche people during this time period. In spite of his busy schedule with the adult education program, Kenneth spent off hours drinking.

Throughout his early adult life, from his days at Cameron College forward, Kenneth drank heavily. Kenneth explained that he consumed alcohol to gain courage and make himself more confident. In addition, he learned to enjoy the feeling he got when he drank. Soon he began drinking every day. Over the years, he explains, "I began to lose my mind." Even though he felt alcohol was hurting his health, he could not stop drinking or prevent his addiction to drink. "My mind was getting affected," he explained, "and it was taking longer when I'd come off from it." At times when Kenneth drank, "I couldn't even carry on a conversation and talk." As he spoke to others, he often lost his train of thought. "I'd forget what I'm talking about, and I knew it was affecting my mind. " At that time, such lapses of memory while engaged in conversation "really concerned me more than anything." He knew he was getting "Red Brain." That is, Kenneth understood that his drinking was taking its toll on his body, especially his brain. He knew that liquor killed brain cells, and he feared for the loss of his memory.

In addition to destroying himself, Coosewoon's behavior harmed his family. He and Doraline had two girls, Rae Lynn and Deanna, and the children grew up knowing their father had a drinking problem. The children and Doraline lived in a family situation which was often dysfunctional and involved tension due to the alcoholism. Many nights, Kenneth would be out drinking by himself or with friends, sometimes getting into fights, committing minor crimes, or disappearing for days. Even during those years, Kenneth realized his actions were ruining his family, but he could not stop drinking. Kenneth remembered that he would see healthy families enjoying being with each other and interacting as a close family unit. He would ask the Grandfather why he could not be normal and have a happy family life. Only with time and dramatic spiritual experiences would he be able to attain a positive family life.

Alcoholics Anonymous and Walking a New Red Road

Kenneth experienced excessive drinking until 1974. He explained that at that time, "I was on a tear of two to three weeks." Kenneth walked on a road near his home on his way to find a drink of gasoline so he could commit suicide. Doraline's brother had decided to help Kenneth stop drinking, so Coosewoon's brother-in-law asked a friend and former alcoholic how he broke his addiction. "That fellow told my brother-in-law that he had joined Alcoholics Anonymous and that's how he stopped drinking." Kenneth's brother-in-law took a day off work and set out to find Kenneth and help him. Doraline's brother found Kenneth in a severe suicidal state. He asked Kenneth to get in the car and go home with him. They went to Walters, Oklahoma, where Acey Oberly, a Kiowa man and friend of the family, explained Alcoholics Anonymous (AA) to Kenneth. He gave Kenneth a book on AA and asked him to read it. Acey was going to an AA group meeting on Monday, and he invited Coosewoon to go with him. Kenneth attended the AA meeting and he liked it. He joined a Native American AA group and found immediate help. Kenneth found the AA group a huge asset, and he had previously stopped drinking for two years in

1962 only to relapse. In the meantime, Kenneth lost his job at Fort Sill and began his work as a dry cleaner.

After two years of sobriety, Kenneth felt he deserved a few beers. That started him on a new path of drinking and severe alcoholism. Kenneth lost his dry cleaning business and worked at various jobs. Since he liked to fight and take on many opponents, he became a bouncer in a bar where he received many rewards for his work, including free drinks. This behavior proved disastrous for Kenneth and his family, as he entered a new era of compulsive drinking. Kenneth continued to drink heavily and impair his own life until he became so incapacitated, he ended up in the hospital. On some days, Coosewoon became so ill with alcoholism that he saw Little People at his home and sometimes he got caught up in spider webs that had control of him like Jonathan Swift's Little People that took control of Gulliver during his travels. From 1964 to 1974, Kenneth entered his second phase of alcohol and drug abuse. "I disgraced my family, and I often wondered why I could not be normal."

Kenneth kept drinking until he could no longer control himself. He ruined his health, destroying his liver and other internal organs. He needed a liver transplant and a new life free of drugs and alcohol. Even Coosewoon believed, "I was not going to come out of it." At one point, he was drinking a gallon jug of cheap wine but became so inebriated he could not bring the wine jug to his mouth. While lying on the floor on his back, he begged Doraline to pour the wine into his mouth. Rather than consent, she called an ambulance to take Kenneth to the Indian hospital in Lawton where several health care providers, including Richard Downey, took control of Kenneth and strapped him to a gurney. Doraline believed her husband's best chance was to be committed to the hospital where medical and counseling professionals could help Kenneth. Kenneth had the DTs and acted like a mad man. He went wild in the hospital, tossing orderlies, doctors, and nurses about. His violent actions led Downey and the doctors to use a straitjacket and strap him down in his hospital bed. Kenneth felt mentally unbalanced but with time, his senses returned. He reported, "it took me two weeks to come back to my mind."

Downey admitted Kenneth to the hospital, but that did not end his association with the Comanche man. With time, Downey and Coosewoon became friends. They have maintained a life-long friendship and respect. In fact, Downey helped Kenneth leave alcohol behind and begin a new life in a positive direction. He also became an advocate of Kenneth Coosewoon. Downey helped Kenneth become a leader in the field of alcohol and drug treatment among Native Americans.

Coosewoon remembered this era as a time when he asked God why he could not be normal. At times, Kenneth cried uncontrollably, asking for spiritual help. "One day," Kenneth explained, "I saw a man playing with his children, and I asked God why I can't be like that." Kenneth explained that he was "in bad shape" at this time of his life and "almost lost my mind." He had developed cirrhosis of the liver and was often ill. "I looked like I was 100 years old," Kenneth once commented, adding, "I did not know what I was doing." He admitted, "the only time I could feel good was when I was drinking, or thought I felt good when I was drinking." This was a time in his life when "I got into a lot of trouble." His trouble stemmed from alcoholism, and doctors at the Indian hospital said that Kenneth was going to die from drinking. He displayed many types of risky behavior by fist fighting, wild driving, stealing, and running from law enforcement officers.

During our oral history sessions, Kenneth remembered this time of his life as extremely chaotic and difficult as he made the transition permanently away from drug and alcohol abuse. "I wasn't really scared of death that much," Coosewoon said years later. But his awareness of his condition grew every day. So did his desire to stop drinking forever, which proved to be the first step toward total sobriety and living a life as a healer. From his days in college until January 9, 1974, Coosewoon had lived a rough life due to daily drinking in excess until he could not stop. Sometimes Kenneth went on a "bender" that lasted days and weeks. When Doraline placed him in a hospital, she initiated a highly significant step toward Kenneth's total recovery. To this day, Coosewoon is thankful for her gift to him, which changed his life forever.

Spiritual Visitations

Coosewoon remained in the hospital for days, and the hospital became a learning space where Kenneth began his life transition from alcoholism to sobriety. In his past he had some religious experiences, but his hospital experience in January 1974 proved life-saving and life-changing. During his stay in the hospital, a healing space, Kenneth experienced many spiritual events that are well known and accepted within the American Indian communities of the Native Universe. However, the events Coosewoon described are unfamiliar to many non-Native people, especially in a secular world. But Coosewoon often explained that the Old and New Testaments of the Bible contained many stories of spiritual gifts and miracles. The Bible also contained stories of spiritual visitations from angels and other entities, but modern people have difficulty believing these visitations could take place today.

Native American peoples have a lengthy heritage of spiritual visitations and messages from the Spirit world. Historically, Coosewoon's religious experiences fit into the milieu of Native American prophets and visionaries from Neolin to Tenskwatawa, Handsome Lake, Smohalla, Kennekuk, Wovoka, and Black Elk. Thus, Coosewoon's descriptions of his visitations from the Spirit fit into the ancient motif of indigenous peoples of the Americas and other parts of the world. While he was a patient at the Indian hospital in Lawton, Kenneth experienced many lessons in a Native way. For example, while strapped to his bed, Little People visited him to ridicule and teach him. They certainly conveyed their images and messages to him, and Kenneth took them to heart. In the American Indian world, Little People serve as teachers, advisors, and pests. Little People visited Kenneth while he was strapped to the gurney, and some Little People floated out of the lights above Kenneth's bed, appearing like little space men and dropping down through the dim light descending like feathers down to his bed. Other Little People sat around his bed and on the dresser in his hospital room, laughing and poking fun at Kenneth for acting such a fool by drinking alcohol and making himself sick. They clearly conveyed their message to Coosewoon.

Among many American Indian tribes, people believe that Little People exist on earth. Little People have power to do positive or negative things, but they often bring messages. Each tribe has their own name for Little People, but many believe they live in the environment, especially hills and mountains, hidden from others and appear to individuals on an "as need" basis. Little People appeared to Coosewoon to make fun of him and encourage a change of behavior. Coosewoon reported he saw Little People throughout his stay in the hospital still strapped to his bed, and even after he had begun to recover.

For Coosewoon, Little People were a real part of his transformation from alcoholism to sobriety. At first, Kenneth thought the Little People were hallucinations, but as the years have passed, he is convinced today they were tiny spirit people sent to the hospital by the Creator to force him to change his behavior. He claims he saw the Little People in his hospital room sitting on the edge of a tall chest of drawers. The Little People had a raucous time laughing at Kenneth, pointing their fingers and making fun of him in his awful state. According to Kenneth, "they laughed and laughed at me, poking fun of me and my sorry condition." In addition to the Little People, and far more important, a Spirit visited Kenneth and stood at the foot of his bed.

According to Kenneth Coosewoon, a mist floated into the room from under the door. It appeared as a mist or fog but ultimately took the form of an American Indian elder. Coosewoon identified the entity as a Spirit, a powerful Spirit that took human form and spoke to him. The Spirit stood at the head of the bed and addressed Kenneth directly. Kenneth wondered if the Spirit was a hallucination, but the entity spoke to him, using his name, and gave him a charge. In his own words, Kenneth explained the visitation. "One night," Kenneth remembered, "something came to the foot of my bed like a mist." At first Coosewoon could not see what was there, but with time, it came into view and took human form.

Coosewoon said that as soon as the mist appeared, he felt "something or someone was at the foot of my bed."

With difficulty, Kenneth saw the figure. He remembered blinking his eyes and trying to see through the haze. He saw the mist take the form of a "figure" standing there and it slowly materialized into a human form. It came into better view. A male Spirit person manifested himself at the foot of the bed and spoke directly to Kenneth. The Spirit addressed Coosewoon, saying, "Kenneth you quit drinking now and you'll live to wear out many blue jeans, but if you drink one more time, that'll be it and you'll never make it." In other words, the Spirit told Coosewoon to stop drinking immediately or face death. Kenneth took the advice seriously, deciding to never take a drink again, and he thought long and hard about the Spirit that had come to him. Today, Coosewoon has no doubt that "it was the Great Spirit," the Grandfather, Creator, or God, whatever term one wishes to use to identify the Almighty Master of Life. "But then," Kenneth explained, "I didn't know because I thought I was still hallucinating . . . but today, I know it was Him because I found out it was him." Future events proved to Kenneth the Grandfather had visited him in the hospital to set him on a new path of sobriety and spirituality.

At first, Kenneth told no one about the Spirit visitation, believing people would not believe him. However, over the years, Kenneth has told many people, groups, and children the identity of the Spirit that changed his life, challenged him, and set him on the road to recovery. Coosewoon did not know what to make of the figure for many months after the visitation, but he heeded the words: "if you quit drinking now, you'll live to wear out many blue jeans." The Spirit had admonished Coosewoon to quit drinking, and it seemed the spiritual world had other plans for Kenneth's life. Clearly, drinking alcohol would play no part in his future life, but Kenneth did not know how to interpret the spiritual visitation. After the visitation, the Spirit vanished but Kenneth was to hear the voice of the Spirit in the future and continue to learn from the spiritual world.

Great Spirit Counselor and New Directions

At the time, Kenneth did not know what to think or say about the visitation, and he told no one for four or five years about the appearance of the Spirit. At the time he did not know how to name the visitor or interpret the feelings the Spirit had created inside Kenneth's mind. Kenneth heard from the Spirit again on another occasion when he had to go to the hospital. The Spirit asked Kenneth if he was ready to pass over into the next world. Without hesitation, Kenneth had answered the Spirit voice: "No Grandfather," Coosewoon explained, "there's some things I need to do, that I want to do before I'm ready to go." The Spirit told Kenneth that this was not his time to pass over.

The Spirit brought clarity to Kenneth's mind and a realization that he was a part of a much larger world system of seen and unseen forces. In addition, the Spirit brought physical healing as Kenneth's liver and other vital organs began to regenerate. In reality, Kenneth received new organs, including a new liver free of scar damage. The non-surgical replacement—his renewed liver—was symbolic of his renewed life on earth. From that time in 1974 forward, Kenneth became more informed about his own health and well-being, including his mental attitude toward himself and others. He also took greater stock in his own Indian identity and began learning more about American Indian ways and culture, especially the religious beliefs of several tribes including his own. Kenneth became open to his Native American heritage, a process that grew gradually after the Spirit visitation and message about entering the Spirit world.

During one interview in 2011, Coosewoon proclaimed, "I know now, it was the Great Spirit, the Grandfather Creator, coming to tell me to end my drinking and become a productive man." Over time, "I found out it was Him. But at the time, I did not know for sure. I told no one about the Spirit and messages for years." Kenneth had to make sense of the visitation in his own mind first before he could share this vision with others. But his visit with the Creator did not end in the hospital. The hospital visitation and messages given to Kenneth was the first of many direct encounters with the Creator Spirit, the Grandfather of mankind. Thus, the hospital visitation was not the last time the Grandfather made himself known to Kenneth. Over time, occasionally and through prayer, Kenneth explained that the Creator would visit and speak with him, bringing new insights and messages that further changed Kenneth's life and helped others. The Spirit vision in the hospital proved to be just the beginning.

After drinking many years and recovering in the hospital, Kenneth returned home to Medicine Park where he began a new life. Since that time, he has never taken a drink and has lived his life helping others. Once again, he rejoined Alcoholics Anonymous with a group of other Native Americans, and he began walking "the Good Red Road." This is a phrase Kenneth has used for many years and continues to use today. It is a common term used by contemporary American Indians to describe their lives as Native Americans without drugs and alcohol. The phrase also indicates that a person is following a traditional Indian way of life, attempting every day to walk with the Creator on a good path without drugs and alcohol. The Good Red Road is tied to a return to Native American spiritualism and traditional Native American ways of life. Kenneth's hospital stay and the Spirit visitation encouraged him to look at himself, look within his soul about who he was and what he was doing on earth. Kenneth became "introspective" and began "finding his faults" and "working on them."

Most significant, Kenneth left his ego behind and did some soul searching to investigate his hatred of others. He investigated his own personality to interrogate his "resentment, envy, jealousy, everything you've got to work on" to become a better human being. The experience brought sobriety and renewal for Coosewoon who has remained sober for over forty years. During that time, Kenneth "was happy" but he felt unfulfilled and still searching for something significant in his life. "I was alright," he reported, "but there was still something I was seeking for, looking for, searching for." For all those years, he "didn't know what it was," but some years later, after learning the Sweat Lodge Ceremony, he realized the meaning of his life on earth.

However, the Sweat Lodge Ceremony did not come into Kenneth's life immediately after returning from the hospital. It was four years away, four being a sacred number to Comanche and Kiowa people. He had "no thought of running the Sweat Lodge Ceremony." But Kenneth stopped drinking and began walking in the light of the Spirit, which guided his life. That same Spirit has been a part of his life ever since (actually, all his life), and Kenneth openly and generously shared his experiences with anyone interested in listening and learning. Like the ancient heroes of Native American oral literature, Kenneth Coosewoon began living a life to benefit others, not himself. He put self-interest behind him and began a new journey on the Good Red Road.

Alcohol and Drug Abuse Counselor and First Sweat Lodge Ceremony

When Coosewoon returned home from the hospital, he "sobered up because I was scared." He also spent more time with his family, attempting to re-establish positive relations with Doraline, his girls, friends, and relatives. He began a new life abstaining from alcohol, and his negative experiences as an alcoholic led him into the field of substance abuse prevention and cause. He wanted to help other drug and alcohol addicts. Psychologist Richard Downey had treated Coosewoon when he was in the hospital, and he grew to have great confidence in Kenneth's ability to run a treatment center for Native Americans. He hired Kenneth to run an alcohol and abuse program at the old Fort Sill Indian School. He placed great trust in Kenneth when he asked the Comanche man to direct the program, but Downey had faith as well that Coosewoon would do an excellent job. And he did. Kenneth understood the responsibility placed in him by Downey, Doraline, and others. He had no desire to disappoint anyone or return to his old ways of drinking.

To help him with his commitment to sobriety, Kenneth continued attending Alcoholics Anonymous meetings, and joined an all-Native American group of men from the Lawton area. Together, this group conducted many activities. In June 1978, he became an alcohol and drug counselor for the Public Health Service at the Lawton Indian Hospital where he counseled other Indian alcoholics. Downey, the man that helped Kenneth overcome his own alcohol problem, helped Kenneth become a program director. Kenneth had immediate success working with Indian alcoholics, as they could relate to him. Since he was an alcoholic, a Comanche, and had experienced the horrors of alcohol and drug abuse and the benefits of sobriety, Coosewoon understood the problems other American Indian people faced and their difficulty when trying to abstain from alcohol.

Kenneth developed preventive education for Indians with substance issues. He especially helped young Indian people. He formulated a successful recovery plan for each individual "in accordance with his or her immediate and long-range goals." Coosewoon used an adaptive model course of recovery drawing on methods used by Alcoholics Anonymous. Finally, Coosewoon began setting up programs within the schools that served Native Americans, making a special effort to teach young people about substance abuse. Kenneth's program blossomed into a successful prevention program, and other administrators in Oklahoma began seeking his advice for their programs. Kenneth was clean and sober by 1978, and he changed his life to help others. Still, he recalled, "there was something missing."

From 1978 to 1989, Kenneth became the Executive Director of the Drop-In Center in Lawton, an American Indian substance abuse program supported by the Bureau of Indian Affairs. He expanded this program in 1989 with a grant from the federal government. Kenneth administered a highly successful program for Native Americans. His program worked out of the old Fort Sill Indian School, and

Kenneth had clients from many diverse tribes. He expanded his approach and methods of dealing with Indians with substance abuse problems, and he worked with several tribal governments in Oklahoma, social service programs, and various levels of government to enhance his program. While he administered the Drop-In Center at the former Indian school, Kenneth first became familiar with the Sweat Lodge Ceremony.

In this photograph, Kenneth tends the fire that heats the rocks. In 1978, he was tending such a fire at Dwight Mission along Sallisaw Creek when the fire cracked and shot forth blue glowing charcoal that became his Blue Medicine, thus beginning the Great Vision that changed his life and led him to lead the Sweat Lodge Ceremony.

When Kenneth was a boy, he saw neighbors with Sweat Lodges in their back yards, but he knew little about ceremonies associated with Sweat Lodge Ceremonies. In his youth, his family had nothing to do with Sweat Lodge Ceremonies. "My mother was real religious," Coosewoon once said, "but she never told me anything about the Sweat

Lodge." Years later, Kenneth learned that his mother's father, a Kiowa man, had led the Sweat Lodge Ceremony to help and heal other people. The old Kiowa grandfather had once kept a Sweat Lodge on the very property where Kenneth was raised, but the elder had died before Kenneth was born, and he did not know of his family's previous connection to the land.

Kenneth's Kiowa mother, was raised in Oklahoma by traditional people. Her relatives were medicine people and social elites within the tribal communities. They had lived to help others. However, Kenneth's mother did not raise him in a traditional manner, and she did not teach him the medicine ways of Kiowa people. In fact, she made it a point to keep her children away from traditional medicine ways, believing that her children should not be exposed too deeply to Native American culture, which could harm their ability to be a part of the dominant society. Kenneth grew up among both Comanche and Kiowa people and learned generally about the cultural, healing, and spiritual ways of both people, but his mother kept him from ceremonies and healings for another reason. Since she had become a Christian, she shielded her children from Native American spiritual beliefs and ceremony, which some Christians considered heathenism. Thus, his mother did not expose him to Kiowa or Comanche medicine in any formal manner. She wanted Kenneth raised as a Christian with a future, and in her mind, this future had to be devoid of American Indian culture and religion that held children back in the general population of Oklahoma and the United States.

Mattie's views of Native American culture and religion resulted from the successful efforts of Christian reformers in and out of the United States government. For many years, Christian ministers and agents sought the forced assimilation and Christianization of Native Americans, which had a huge impact within the Indian communities of the United States. Mattie Kauley was not alone in her attitudes about the place of Native American religious beliefs in modern society. Many Native American parents of the twentieth century believed they had to protect their children against the future by encouraging them to discard the old Indian beliefs and customs to embrace modernity and Christ. Like other parents, she refused to teach Kenneth and his siblings about the language, religion, and medicine ways of Kiowa or Comanche people. To do so, she believed, would be an impediment to her children.

Thus, Mattie raised Kenneth in the Kiowa Methodist Church, away from Kiowa and Comanche medicine ways. In her mind, to raise children within Native culture would be a violation of the teachings of Christ. Kiowa and Comanche had long believed in the healing power of the Creator, the divine power that placed the first human beings on earth. Comanche and Kiowa had rich oral narratives about the Creation and the laws established at the beginning of time. But many Christians, especially Christian fundamentalist leaders in the so-called "Bible Belt," believed that Indian spirituality constituted the counter image of Christ. Some Christian ministers viewed and taught their parishioners that Comanche and Kiowa spiritual medicine was evil and dangerous. Kenneth's mother accepted these negative views of American Indian religious beliefs, and she prevented Kenneth from learning about their Native spiritual, culture, religion, and healing. He would learn the Native American ways, especially medicine ways, in years to come, particularly from his future friends and mentors, Wallace and Gracie Black Elk.

As a boy, Coosewoon had enjoyed a real sense of his Indian identity, but he wanted to be popular with girls, play sports, and one day own a car. In his mind, this would make him a "big man" and attract beautiful women eager to be with a Native American athlete. As a result, he abandoned most of his Indian identity and had little interest in traditional indigenous culture. Today Coosewoon laments the fact that his mother "liked the old culture," but "she got into Christianity then she never taught anything or said much about" Kiowa or Comanche culture. Still, she held onto some aspects of traditional Kiowa life, including the intricate and beautiful art form of Plains Indian beadwork. Kenneth's mother was a master artist in beadwork, and she made many beautiful art objects for people. She gave away and sold many items to other Indians and non-Indians, using the funds to pay for extras for her family. Kenneth regretted he was not raised with knowledge of spiritual healing and traditional power. In his own words, he put it this way: "My folks knew about the Sweat Lodge," he explained, "because they had one right down here [Medicine Park] for the old people, but after my mother got religion, she never told us anything about the Sweat Lodge."

Kenneth's father influenced the course of Kenneth's life by being a positive role model. He taught Kenneth elements of family history, including the family's role in the past as superior warriors. Kenneth's father was Comanche, raised in southwestern Oklahoma north of the Red River. He was born into a family known for its great warriors, many of whom had fought the United States in the nineteenth century after tribal commerce and trade had spread widely across the American West. Like his mother, Kenneth's father refused to raise his children in the spiritual traditions of Comanche people, believing it would not benefit the children to keep up the old ways. Coosewoon's father felt that Comanche culture would prove a detriment to his son's future progress in school, business, and life in general.

As a result of Abner's views, Kenneth's father did not teach him many things about the cultural and spiritual ways of Comanche people. He felt it best to shield him from future abuse, ostracism, and racism by not educating him about the Comanche way of life and being. Coosewoon did not grow up deep in his own culture or that of other Native Americans. As Ted Vaughn, a Yavapai elder once explained, "they took that away from us." The dominant society denigrated Comanche culture and language to such a degree that Indian parents raising their children during the early and mid- twentieth century did not teach their traditional culture to young people. In addition, schoolteachers did not emphasize the positive elements of Native American culture or teach Comanche, Kiowa, or Plains Indian cultures. They often silenced Native American history so it would be lost and forgotten. Parents sometimes turned away from their rich cultural beliefs, believing they were helping their children survive in a new world order dominated by white Americans. Parents sometimes believed familial emphasis on Native culture was a disservice to Indian children forced to interact with non-Indians. Unlike Native Americans living in remote areas of the United States, Comanche and Kiowa of Oklahoma lived in close proximity to non-Indian farmers, ranchers, merchants, military, and oil workers from various towns of southwestern Oklahoma, especially Lawton, Oklahoma.

Kenneth grew up knowing more about the Peyote Religion and the Native American Church than the Sweat Lodge. Several Comanche and Kiowa neighbors participated in the Native American Church or Peyote Church. Kenneth grew up knowing Nelson and Harding Big Bow, for example, as well as other people participating in the Native American Church. Kenneth had attended meetings of the Native American Church, entering the tipi, praying, and singing all night in ceremony. He remembered the speeches of various leaders of the Native American Church. "They never denigrated other people or religions," Kenneth explained, "and they always emphasized that many paths led to the Grandfather."

Leaders of the Native American Church argued that people are free to choose which trail they wished to take, as many led paths to the Almighty. "I listened to them pray," Kenneth recalled, "and they never downed anybody." Kenneth appreciated "the way they prayed" and never said "you're going to go to Hell" if you act this way or another. "You never heard them ever say things against Christians or any other religion," Coosewoon said. In fact, some members of the Native American Church also attended Christian churches. Harding Big Bow once reported to me that in the morning after a Peyote Church meeting, Jesus appeared to all the participants, walking on a cloud overhead of the group while eating breakfast. Harding reported, "this was a good sign." About the Native American Church, Coosewoon stated, "They never said negative stuff like that in their Peyote meetings, and they never tried to force you into their religion or their way of thinking." Leaders of the Peyote Church welcomed Kenneth, "if you want to go, and if you don't, . . . well that's ok too." Coosewoon grew up knowing about the Native American Church but he never joined. He learned nothing about the Sweat Lodge Ceremony as a young person, even though Kiowa and Comanche had practiced the Sweat

Lodge religion before they had accepted the Peyote religion.

Kenneth did not experience the Sweat Lodge until adulthood. As a young man, Coosewoon had little interest in learning about Native American culture, history, or language. "I just never was interested in our Indian history," he once confided. He did not venture deeply into the Native American Church, pow wow competitions, or ancient songs and stories of the Indian people of southwestern Oklahoma. His interest in learning about Native American traditions came years later, after the Spirit visited him in the hospital. It took him years to learn more about his own identity as a Native American living in the late twentieth century. His attitude changed dramatically after his last ambulance ride to the hospital. Over many years, Kenneth had attempted suicide several times. He always failed. He had felt a failure in many areas of life, as a professional, husband, father, and community member. Today, Kenneth believes the Grandfather who had greater plans for Coosewoon spared him death.

For many years prior to his Spirit visitation, people that knew Kenneth believed he would die in the hospital or in a violent manner brought on by himself or others with a grudge against him. His friends and family knew he had ruined his liver, which was in horrible shape. He needed a new liver, surgery and an organ transplant, but this option was not available to Kenneth who continued to drink. However, Coosewoon explained that his personal transformation took place as a result of his "forced removal to the emergency room," which "saved my life and put me on a new path." His hospitalization revitalized his body and spirit on many levels and eventually gave him a new reason to live and purpose in life.

Kenneth's world changed in many ways after the Grandfather visited him in the hospital, including his newfound interest in his own Native American identity and indigenous cultures of the Great Plains. After his discharge from the hospital, he began a journey into his own Comanche and Kiowa cultures as well as the cultural and historical world of many Native American tribes. He ultimately learned a great deal about Lakota history and culture. His visitation also led ultimately led to the Sweat Lodge Ceremony. In that way, he has continued an ancient tradition used by Plains Indians and others across the Native Universe.

He began reading works by and about Native Americans, including Black Elk, Lame Deer, and other medicine people. He grew in his friendship and association with other Indians seeking sobriety through Alcoholics Anonymous. Coosewoon "joined Alcoholics Anonymous and they started me off on the Good Red Road, what Indians call a Good Red Road of sobriety and personal responsibility." For the first time in his life, Kenneth began "looking at myself and within myself." Coosewoon began considering what he could handle or change in his life and those things over which he had little or no control. He tried to ignore issues about which he could not control and focus on those things he could change. He worked hard at being positive toward himself, his family, and his friends. With the help of many others, including his family and friends, he began to use Native American beliefs to change his life. He became "introspective, looking within yourself." He began learning more about traditional Indian ways.

"I looked within myself to see my faults and work on them so I could become a better person." Coosewoon tried hard to identify his faults, hatreds, resentments, envies, and jealousies. For several years, Kenneth attended AA meetings, and he worked diligently to learn more about his Native American heritage. He also began to help others, first through AA and later through Alcohol Treatment Centers in Apache and Lawton, Oklahoma.

After his Great Vision, Kenneth stopped hunting and killing animals. In this photograph, the deer ate from Kenneth's hand. Kenneth has a knack of dealing with animals of all kind, and before he led his first Sweat Lodge Ceremony to pray for the healing of his daughter's boyfriend, many birds circled overhead above the lodge on Cache Creek, which Kenneth took as a good sign.

American Indians occupy an important place in the realm of human society, because most Native Americans can forgive non-Indians, missionaries, and territorial, state, and national governments within the United States for what happened to them in the past. In spite of the physical, spiritual, and mental attacks, and outright genocide on American Indian people, Coosewoon believes that Indian spiritual leaders have looked beyond that ugly and unfortunate past to find goodness and worth among people of all colors and backgrounds. "We're kind to all of God's creation and it doesn't matter the color of your skin or mine. We all have the same blood. We are all people. We are all the same." And as Mohave scholar Michael Tsosie argued, "in comparison to the full length of our history and the depth of our cultures, our relations with the United States is like a small blip on a radar screen. Our lives are much deeper and our cultures are more complex than that."

Still, Kenneth and Rita Coosewoon are well aware of the historical trauma suffered by most American Indians because of actions taken by the federal, territorial, state, and local governments that harmed Native American people throughout American history. They know about these things because they have personally suffered from racism and hatred targeted at American Indian people. In addition, their families experienced terrible events in past centuries. The United States forced many Comanche people into signing the Medicine Lodge Treaty of 1867, and several bands of Comanche fought the United States during the Red River Wars of the 1870s. During the mid-nineteenth century, Comanche and their Native neighbors watched non-Indian buffalo hunters slaughter the bison for their hides. The United States Army encouraged the near extermination of the buffalo, knowing the Plains Indians depended on the buffalo as their central food source. Once the hunters destroyed the buffalo, Comanche, Kiowa, Cheyenne, Ponca, Pawnee, Lakota, Dakota, Ojibway, and many other Indian tribal people starved on various reservations.

In the past, mothers miscarried their babies and

infants died due to malnutrition, parents on reservations watched their children die of cholera, measles, influenza, pneumonia, tuberculosis, and other infectious diseases. Invisible enemies—bacteria and viruses—took the lives of untold numbers of children on reservations and in boarding schools established by the federal government and churches to destroy Native American cultures, languages, and religions. Teachers and administrators at the Fort Sill Indian School in Lawton attempted to break Rita Coosewoon's spirit and her attachment to her culture and language. They failed. She continues strong in Comanche culture, art, and language, having shared her knowledge and talents with her family and youngsters for many years. Neither Rita nor Kenneth has forgotten the historical trauma of their people and that of Native Americans throughout the Native Universe. But they do not allow their knowledge of the trauma to overwhelm their being and harm their belief in the unity of mankind with the Grandfather.

In spite of understanding the historical trauma experienced by Native Americans, the Coosewoons strive daily to set aside negative feelings toward others. They emphasize the positive and they reflect this in their oral histories that continually focus on the unity and oneness of mankind. Kenneth points out that every person on earth is the child of the Creator, Grandfather, Great Spirit, or God. Reverend Sheldon Swick, a Mohave Indian elder and Christian minister from the Colorado River Indian Reservation, confirms Coosewoon's belief in the oneness of mankind. Reverend Swick once explained that Mastahmo, the Mohave Creator, was the same as the Christian God. "They are the same beings, no difference," Reverend Swick once explained, "and we all live under his rule." Although

Swick is a Christian minister, he still acknowledges the power and oneness of the Mohave Creator.

And in a significant book by historian Lisbeth Haas, she points out that in the early nineteenth century, Luiseño Indian scholar Pablo Tac compared his god, Chinigchinich, with the Christian god. Coosewoon agrees that the Supreme Being is one and the same, regardless of the name humans give to the Grandfather Spirit. Many Christian and other religious leaders around the world may object to this view, but several Native American spiritual leaders, including Coosewoon, Swick, and Tac, believe the Creator is one with the universe and all animate and inanimate beings. As scholar Lee Ann Smith-Trafzer has stated, "many roads lead to the Almighty Master of Life." Coosewoon believes the same way. Regardless of the name applied, Grandfather is the same as the Almighty, Creator, and God. For many people, one God or Creator exists and looks over all of mankind and all things in the universe regardless of a person's faith. This is the belief Coosewoon takes into the Sweat Lodge, and he insists that people participating in the ceremony keep an open mind during the ceremony whether or not they agree with him about the oneness of Grandfather.

Learning and Building the Sweat Lodge

When Kenneth began his tenure as Director of the Drop-In Center Drug and Alcohol Center in Lawton, two of his clients selected a site in Cache Creek to build a Sweat Lodge. At that time, Kenneth knew virtually nothing about the ceremony and its purpose. Eventually he would learn about the ceremony in detail. Since his release from the hospital and his days of self-analysis, Kenneth knew he was recovering. "But something was missing in my life cause I was searching for it, feeling it." Coosewoon said, "I did not know until later" that "I needed the Sweat Lodge and needed to use it to help others." However, at the time, he did not know about the meaning of the Sweat Lodge or how to use it to help others. In many ways, building the Sweat Lodge on Cache Creek began a major transformation that led him into healing.

A few of the clients at the Center said, "Kenneth, we found a good place to build a Sweat Lodge." They planted the seed for the treatment center to supplement other forms of healing with the Sweat Lodge Ceremonies. The men and others became enthusiastic about building a Sweat Lodge near the school right off Cache Creek. Kenneth agreed to help build the Sweat Lodge, and together, the men set out to construct a lodge with willows. Although Kenneth had heard of Sweat Lodges, he thought people used them to sweat in order to lose weight. He soon learned that the Sweat Lodge had far greater meaning as a "little church" for Indian people, a sacred space that brought people closer to the Creator. Soon, Kenneth learned that the Sweat Lodge offered many forms of healing.

Kenneth helped his clients with the first Sweat Lodge for the treatment center. "I helped them build one," Coosewoon confided. "And one of my clients led the first Sweat Lodge I was ever in." From his clients and other future experiences with the Sweat Lodge, Kenneth learned to create the Sweat Lodge in his own manner. He always emphasized that content, intention, and function were far more important than form. Native Americans use many methods to build the Sweat Lodge, and Kenneth has his own technique. During one oral history, Coosewoon offered great detail about his method of building of a Sweat Lodge. He explained that many varieties of Sweat Lodges exist, depending on the tribe from which they emerged. But Kenneth uses the Sweat Lodge of many tribes of the Great Plains, including the Comanche, Kiowa, and Lakota. His style of Sweat Lodge originated from instructions from Grandfather and his personal experiences.

Gracie Black Elk, the wife of Wallace Black Elk, took special interest in Kenneth and Rita Coosewoon. At one Sweat Lodge Ceremony, Gracie taught him Sweat Lodge songs, even before Kenneth led the ceremony. "That old woman knew something I didn't. She knew that one day, I would lead sweats, so she gave me her songs, which I still sing in the ceremony." Kenneth remembers that Gracie said, "I want to give you these two songs, healing songs." One of the songs is the "Calling the Spirit Song." Gracie gave the song specifically to Kenneth to use in healing ceremonies.

A year after meeting Wallace Black Elk the first time at the Sweat Lodge Ceremony near the Dwight Mission, Coosewoon attended a second ceremony in the Cookson Hills of Oklahoma at the same site as the first one a year before. Wallace brought Gracie to the Cherokee Country for the ceremony, and Gracie continued to form a close relationship with Kenneth and Rita Coosewoon. She told Kenneth, "I'm going to leave here soon, but I will never leave you. I'll always be with you; I'll always be there to teach you; just call on me." Gracie Black Elk told Coosewoon to always "help people and many miracles will happen." Over the years, Gracie has appeared in Sweat Lodge Ceremonies and lectures given by Kenneth. He says her spirit still guides his daily life.

Kenneth Coosewoon constructs the Sweat Lodge in the tradition of Comanche, Lakota, and other people of the Great Plains. Although some Indians place the opening to their Sweat Lodge to the west, Coosewoon always orients his Sweat Lodges to the east, the direction of the dawn, wisdom, and knowledge. Tribal people use a variety of wood to make their Sweat Lodges, but Coosewoon prefers the use of long, thin willow shoots that he collects close to his home. Kenneth and Rita gather willow in a prayerful manner. Kenneth is careful to gather the right willows and not to cut and waste a single stem. He selects the willow that is just the right size that he needs for their use in the sweat. Different people use different numbers of willow poles, but Coosewoon selects a total of 18 willows to cut. He uses 12 on the bottom layer and three on the top, saving the other poles for additional uses. Before leaving the area, Kenneth cleans the willows, stripping them of their bark and preparing them for their use in the lodge. Kenneth and Rita pray before they take the willow, explaining to the plant and Creator why they are taking these "live" trees to live again as elements of a holy ceremony.

They gather their willows near the shore of Lake Lawtonka in southwestern Oklahoma, located near Medicine Park and Lawton, Oklahoma. Not far away, they also gather sacred plants to use in the ceremony, including sage, flat cedar, and red berry cedar. They begin the process of building the Sweat Lodge by locating a level area where they can create small holes in the earth to insert the willow poles. Coosewoon marks off a ten-foot circle using a five-foot piece of string. He stands in the center of the circle and with the string marks the circle with a sharp instrument at the end of the string. In this way, he draws out a circle of 10 feet in circumference. "Then you put two willows at the door facing east, and then you put two at the western side followed by two polls to the north and two to the south."

Coosewoon checks each pole to ensure that it is the correct length and has been placed sufficiently deep into the earth. Then he begins connecting the poles in a ritual manner, bending them to meet their partner pole directly across from it. After placing the willow poles deep into the earth, Coosewoon ties the two poles to the east with those to the west, bending them and tying them near the middle. Coosewoon then ties the posts to the north and south together, beginning the formation of the round Sweat Lodge. In this manner, the leader and assistants work around the lodge, tying poles together to form the circle. To hold the structure together, the leader uses poles to tie horizontally around the lodge, tying each pole bent from the ground to the opposite side to the poles going around the lodge. Those people building the Sweat Lodge often rest after constructing the structure, taking time to relax and contemplate the forthcoming ceremony.

After completing the skeleton of the lodge, Coosewoon digs a hole in the middle of the lodge to hold the hot rocks. When offering a Sweat Lodge Ceremony far from his home, he often takes local reddish-orange cobblestones from home packing them in the trunk of his car. Kenneth and Rita gather rocks together, praying before they take them from the Earth. They explain the purpose for which they are taking them, saying to the rocks that they will be used in the Sweat Lodge Ceremony for healing. Kenneth believes the rocks represent both the earth and fire within the earth, a gift from the Grandfather.

Either before Kenneth digs the hole in the center of the lodge or afterwards, the leader covers the lodge in skins, canvas, cotton blankets, or other materials that will not harm participants when the lodge is heated. They never use plastic

On April 11, 2015, Kenneth Coosewoon conducted a Sweat Lodge Ceremony in his backyard. Prior to this ceremony, Kenneth and Ronald Cooper had cut willows for the lodge and built this frame for it.

because of the intense heat. Often, Coosewoon uses old canvas tents, particularly the heavily oiled tents that hold in heat and steam. Kenneth points out that tribal elders told him that when the rocks are placed in the middle of the lodge floor, the area becomes the center of the universe. Intense heat and fire created the rocks Coosewoon uses in the Sweat Lodge Ceremony, and these rocks hold the fire of life within the universe. The Sweat Lodge is like a miniature universe. In addition to the heated rocks, Coosewoon enters the lodge with a bucket of water, which he uses to pour on the rocks to create steam. He explains the water is life itself, a gift of the Creator, and when used in the Sweat Lodge, it becomes holy water, an extension of the Grandfather that permeates the mind, body, and spirit of participants.

Benefits of Sweat Lodge

Kenneth participated in his first Sweat Lodge Ceremony on Cache Creek not far from the old Fort Sill Boarding School. His Kiowa client led the ceremony and brought Coosewoon into the lodge for the first time. As soon as Coosewoon participated in his first Sweat Lodge Ceremony, he learned immediately that he "liked what I experienced." By helping his clients at the treatment center build the Sweat Lodge, Kenneth learned one method of construction. Kenneth's clients taught him their method of constructing the Sweat Lodge and invited Kenneth into the lodge. When he entered the Sweat Lodge with his clients, he found "peace and goodness" in the ceremony from the very start. "I can tell you this," he exclaimed passionately, "I liked it." When Kenneth entered the Sweat Lodge, he sat on the west side and saw "all my old people." After his first experience in the lodge with his clients, Coosewoon wanted to hire a leader of the Sweat Lodge to provide ceremony for his clients. He believed there was great benefit in the ceremony for people that abused drugs and alcohol, and he believed the form of prayer used in ceremony would help heal his American Indian clients. He felt his clients could relate to the ceremony in a deep and meaningful way, and that the Healing Spirit would help his clients.

In many ways, Coosewoon believed the Sweat Lodge would enhance his alcohol and drug abuse program by offering clients an extension of the Twelve Step Program of Alcoholics Anonymous, which he felt was very effective in helping Indian people and others cope with their disease. Coosewoon sensed that the Sweat Lodge Ceremony would add a new and deeper spiritual dimension to his program and enhance the experiences of those clients attending Alcoholics Anonymous meetings. Kenneth did not attempt to create a new or innovative approach to substance abuse, but he felt that Sweat Lodge would offer some American Indian clients a Native American method of acknowledging their addiction and making progress in defeating the monsters plaguing them.

Kenneth's concept of using the Sweat Lodge to heal people that abused drugs and alcohol was not new in Indian Country. American Indian healers had used the ceremony for this purpose and other forms of healing in the past, but the method may have been new for a treatment center. The concept of using the Sweat Lodge certainly was innovative for Coosewoon who had never conceived of using it in the treatment plan for clients. In the future, other alcohol and drug treatment centers serving Native Americans would follow Kenneth's example and use the Sweat Lodge to help clients. Today, for example, the Friendship House in the Mission District of San Francisco employs a Lakota healer full time and the Indian Center in Oakland also uses the Sweat Lodge to help their clients. American Indian prisoners have also used the Sweat Lodge, which indigenous people have used with success for generations.

When Kenneth first entered the Sweat Lodge on Cache Creek, his knowledge of the sacred space had just begun. But he soon learned a great deal about the Sweat Lodge and its meaning. As Coosewoon gained in his understanding of Sweat Lodge, he began relating it to Comanche heritage and that of the indigenous people of the Great Plains. "Our Sweat Lodge is round, and our tipis are round. We Comanche always put the tipis in a circle, and that's where our strength is, in the circle. The old people say our strength was the round, like the tornado, which is one of the strongest things on Mother Earth. He comes in a circle, so we make our Sweat Lodges in circles." Like the tipi, Plains Indians made (and make) the Sweat Lodge round like nests. The space within the lodge is meant to embrace participants and help patients feel close to the Creator, truly embraced by healing forces. Entering the round Sweat Lodge on hands and knees, the round lodge becomes a symbol of the womb of the earth. The rocks are placed in the center of the lodge providing light, heat, and steam that radiates out from the center of the circle bringing healing. During the Sweat Lodge Ceremony, the heat and steam penetrate the skin, throat, lungs, and all parts of the body, inside and out. The steam and heat bring the Creator directly into the body of all participants.

From his first experience forward, Kenneth developed an understanding of the Sweat Lodge Ceremony, saying the holy space offers "one method of praying and giving thanks to Grandfather, God." Kenneth points out that before 1978 and the passage of the American Indian Religious Freedom Act, "it was against the law" to conduct a Sweat Lodge Ceremony. Indian agents and Indian police could incarcerate Indian people in jail for conducting a ceremony, so Indian peoples "had to go underground to even use the Sweat Lodge."

Native Americans often left more populated areas close to agencies to build Sweat Lodges and conduct ceremonies in secrecy. On all the reservations, Indian people quietly moved temporarily away from non-Indians so they could conduct ceremony and not be harassed. Since his Great Vision, Coosewoon has presented his knowledge of the Sweat Lodge and spiritual healing with thousands of listeners, including students at the University of Oklahoma and the University of California, Riverside. Kenneth believes that his association with the Sweat Lodge is part of the great circle within Native America. Sweat Lodge is just one form of ceremony and indigenous healing. According to Coosewoon, the Sweat Lodge is truly Native to the Americas, a gift of the Grandfather who created the people in the Western Hemisphere and "placed them in their homelands."

Coosewoon believes that Native Americans built their Sweat Lodges on "our holy land." To Kenneth, the entire length of North and South America is holy land. He said that the earth is sacred "cause it is a gift of the Creator." Kenneth feels strongly that the land of his forefathers and other Native Americans is "holy land here" because "this is where the Grandfather placed us." Many other Native Americans proclaim the same message.

In 1855, for example, Yakama Chief Owhi, explained, "the Almighty looked one way and then the other, but he named these lands for us." Kenneth believes the Sweat Lodge was the first way of praying among Native Americans, a place to give thanks to "Grandfather, God." He stated, "at one time, all the Indians had the Sweat Lodge, but through Christianity and over the years, we lost it." He pointed out that agents of the Office of Indian Affairs and Christian missionaries working in Indian country discouraged or outlawed the use of Sweat Lodge Ceremonies, believing it was a pagan act and anti-Christian. But in the late twentieth century, Native American spiritual leaders revived the wider use of the Sweat Lodge Ceremony, encouraging others but especially Native Americans to use the Sweat Lodge for spirituality, psychology, prayers, purification, thanksgiving, counseling, and healing. It is a living, sacred way carried on by many healers. Kenneth Coosewoon was one of many Native Americans who kept the

Sweat Lodge alive and enlarged the circle of its use among Indians and non-Indians in North America.

Toward the Great Vision

Kenneth had attended only one Sweat Lodge Ceremony at the treatment center before attending his second Sweat Lodge Ceremony, not in the heart of Comanche and Kiowa country, but in the land of the Cherokee people of Oklahoma. While working as director of the treatment center at Fort Sill Indian School, Kenneth received an invitation to attend a gathering of Native Americans at Dwight Mission, located in the Cookson Hills of eastern Oklahoma. Coosewoon eagerly attended a retreat with a number of Native American directors of drug and alcohol treatment centers. While he was there, he experienced his second Sweat Lodge Ceremony. This Sweat Lodge Ceremony proved to be highly significant to Coosewoon, offering new sight and vision for him.

From Lawton, Oklahoma, Kenneth drove northeast toward Tulsa, Oklahoma, and into Cherokee Country in eastern Oklahoma. The gathering took place in the wooded hills of Oklahoma at a small community that included the Dwight Mission, a Baptist mission to the Cherokee. The mission sits on the edge of a thick wood on the top of a small hill above Sallisaw Creek winding its way out of a meadow into the forest. Kenneth's journey to Dwight Mission proved to be one of the most significant and dramatic adventures in his life. It would turn out to be Coosewoon's pathway into Native American healing through the Sweat Lodge Ceremony. Directors of Native treatment centers and Alcoholics Anonymous gathered for a workshop at the Dwight Mission

in the Cookson Hills of the Cherokee Country of eastern
Oklahoma.

For many years, Baptists had operated a Christian
church and school for Cherokee children at Dwight Mission.
The mission touched the lives of many Cherokee people
and their neighbors. The site was ideal for a workshop and
Sweat Lodge Ceremony for the directors. From the two-lane
highway, the Church sits back from the road and is nestled
in a grove of thick woods. Sloping down from the mission,
church officials created a cemetery for parishioners and
children that had died while attending school. Still farther
below the backside of the mission runs Sallisaw Creek, which
winds its way through a cleared valley before snaking its
way behind the mission and into thick woods. Below the
cemetery, not far from the creek, the directors camped and
built a Sweat Lodge in preparation of a series of ceremony.

Wallace Black Elk and his wife, Gracie Black Elk, led
the Sweat Lodge Ceremony at the Dwight Mission in 1978.
Some of the organizers had asked the Black Elks to lead the
Sweat Lodge, and they invited all the participants into the
sacred space to seek knowledge and healing. For Kenneth,
this was his second Sweat Lodge Ceremony and first with
the renowned Native American healer and his wife. Both
Wallace and Gracie were famous within the Native American
communities of the United States and Canada. They had
chosen the path of helping and healing people through the
Sweat Lodge, and they were open to helping people like
Kenneth find their way to the Spirit. Both Wallace and Gracie
saw something special in Kenneth, especially Gracie who first
shared songs with Kenneth before he even contemplated
leading a Sweat Lodge. In the near future, Wallace also
shared knowledge and songs with Kenneth, assisting him on

his journey into the Spirit. They contributed to Coosewoon's confidence and knowledge of song and ceremony.

This experience led to Kenneth's Great Vision, one of the most life-changing events in his life. Wallace and Gracie recognized early in their relationship with the Coosewoons that one day Kenneth would be a healer and leader of the Sweat Lodge even before Kenneth had his Great Vision. Gracie insisted that Kenneth accept a tape recording of some of the sacred songs they sang during healing ceremonies. Kenneth and Rita eventually became close personal friends with the Black Elks. They gave Kenneth the Chanupa Song, which Kenneth would use in the future.

At the time of the gift, Kenneth had no intention of using the song in a Sweat Lodge or any other ceremony. He could not see himself leading the Sweat Lodge until he experienced the Great Vision during this camp out. Since that time, Kenneth has used the Chanupa and other songs thousands of times. He also learned protocols and procedures of the Sweat Lodge Ceremony that best fit his view of how to conduct healing ceremonies. Over the years, Coosewoon drew on his own experiences and things taught him by the Creator Grandfather to enhance his ceremony. He also drew on his experiences with Wallace and Gracie Black Elk and used their songs. Significantly, he adapted his ceremony to the needs of his participants, following general principles followed by many Plains Indian people.

Kenneth Coosewoon grew into the Sweat Lodge Ceremony slowly, adapting procedures through experience, trial, and error. The Grandfather taught him how to act and offer the Sweat Lodge. During the Great Vision, the Grandfather told Kenneth He would always be with him and that all things he would need in the Sweat Lodge would come to him. And so it has come to pass. Over the years people have given Coosewoon eagle feathers, tobacco, sage, a drum, an eagle bone whistle, buffalo skull, prayer stick, and sacred pipe. He uses these gifts in his healing ceremonies to help others. But all this unfolded after the Great Vision, which began with a Sweat Lodge Ceremony led by Wallace Black Elk down by the Sallisaw Creek that flows near the Dwight Mission.

Visions Within the Sweat Lodge

One afternoon the men prepared for the ceremony by helping Wallace and Gracie build the lodge in a little clearing near the flowing stream. They situated the sacred lodge at the edge of the woods, just downhill from the school's cemetery. They built a fire and began heating the rocks they would use in the ceremony. After a few hours, the rocks became glowing hot and Wallace took them into the center of the lodge and began the religious ceremony with song and prayer. During the Sweat Lodge Ceremony with Wallace and Gracie Black Elk, Kenneth "experienced everything" he "didn't know existed," including "moving spirits" and "sparks that jumped around in the darkness of the Sweat Lodge." Coosewoon thought someone in the Sweat Lodge was striking a cigarette lighter, striking the flint down with his thumb and creating sparks in the total darkness inside the lodge. Kenneth recalled, "the sparks started dancing all around me."

Soon after he saw the sparks or moving spirit and through the darkness, Kenneth witnessed an old rawhide rattle dancing around him. At first, Coosewoon thought one of the other participants was shaking the rattle filled with small rocks or seeds, but he soon realized that no one was shaking the rattle. No one held or manipulated the rattle as it moved about Coosewoon's body suspended in the air. It acted on its own, moving about Coosewoon's body in space and shaking as if someone had control of the instrument, using it to cleanse the area around the Comanche participant. Kenneth heard the beat of the rattle shaking in front of his face. For Coosewoon, the sound of the rattle "was the most beautiful thing I had ever heard." He knew the rattle had spiritual meaning, which seemed to act in concert with the moving spirits or sparks. Today, he believes that the Spirit was using the moving sparks and the rattle to cleanse the area around and within him, bringing his senses into the healing circle of human kind. The spiritual activities were also preparing him for a greater prayer and vision of self. In addition to experiencing moving spirits and a shaking rattle, Kenneth witnessed other spiritual events that became a prelude to even greater experiences that same evening.

During the course of the ceremony, Kenneth fixed his eyes on the red glowing rocks in the middle of the lodge. Something in the center of the rocks caught his eyes, as he reported seeing an unusual spark or beam of light. "I looked down at the rocks," he pointed out, and he "could see a little spark down in the rocks." Kenneth kept looking at the spark and soon a light came out of the rocks, casting a light beam at him "just like a flashlight pen." The long narrow light flashed out of the rocks and streamed in a narrow line from the rocks aimed at Coosewoon's heart. At the time, Kenneth felt the light penetrated his heart and soon he saw "blood spurting out of my chest." Although blood squirted out of his heart each time his heart beat, he felt no pain and wondered if this was symbolic of the spirit world "flushing out my meanness." He thought that the Spirit was cleaning his blood, pushing out the evil, meanness, and negative energy that human's carry with them.

Coosewoon thought everyone could see the light emanating from the center of the lodge. Kenneth sat in the lodge thinking everyone saw the moving spirits, shaking rattle, piercing light, and blood spurting from his heart. In fact, he learned this was not the case. Only Kenneth saw the stream of light beaming out of the rocks and onto his heart. Then Coosewoon asked the man sitting next to him if he could see the light. The man confessed that he did not see the light, but after Coosewoon asked him to move closer and look carefully, the man remarked, "Yeah, it's shining right on your heart." An eagle also appeared in the Sweat Lodge and came to Coosewoon, bringing Kenneth blessings with each movement of his wings. The many visions made Kenneth feel like he was floating. Although somewhat confused by the spiritual messages, Coosewoon felt wonderful while he participated in ceremony inside the Sweat Lodge.

"Spiritually, I felt clean and good," Kenneth said, adding that with time he felt that the events were life-changing. In symbolic ways he was receiving profound messages to change his way of life and to begin life anew, walking the Good Red Road. Coosewoon compared his experience in Black Elk's Sweat Lodge Ceremony with that of Christians who say they can be reborn into their religion by attending a revival meeting. Coosewoon experienced the Sweat Lodge Ceremony that changed his life forever. His spiritual experiences humbled him and taught him a new way, a continuation of the Good Red Road. Inside a sacred lodge built on the Mother Earth in the woods of the Cookson

Hills, a Comanche took a giant step in his transformation into a world of healing and caring for others.

The Great Vision

At dusk during the course of the Sweat Lodge Ceremony, Kenneth volunteered to take care of the fire outside the lodge. While the rest of the men walked up to the mission to have supper, Coosewoon kept close watch over the fire, which was burning brightly and heating the rocks used during the ceremony. As in most ceremonies, the leader of the ceremony brought glowing hot rocks into the lodge and poured water onto the rocks, creating a great amount of steam. In order to keep the rocks hot for the next round in the Sweat Lodge, Coosewoon remained at the campsite to keep the fire going. He also watched over the fire to prevent the fire from spreading into the nearby woods and prairie. After everyone had left the site, Kenneth stood close to the warm fire, often leaning on a shovel or using the shovel to move the burning logs into a better position. While preparing to put more wood on the flames, the fire exploded sending out blue embers. One of the blue embers caught Coosewoon's eye, and he heard a clear voice telling him to pick up the glowing blue ember. This was the beginning of a remarkable experience that developed as a Great Vision and origin of the Blue Medicine Kenneth uses in his healing ceremonies.

When Kenneth heard the voice instruct him to pick up the blue ember, he walked to the glowing charcoal he had first noticed. He knew that normally such sparks bursting from the fire glowed red in the dark, especially when the wind brushed against the ember. But these embers shone bright and blue in the twilight. Kenneth stood over one of the blue glowing embers, "I kept looking at it" and the glowing ember "kept getting brighter and brighter." Something or someone spoke to Kenneth, telling him to pick up one of the hot embers. "When I first picked it up, "Kenneth explained, "it felt like a little bit hot and I started to throw it back down." However, the blue ember cooled to his touch, but kept glowing a deep blue in color. It glowed brighter and brighter, symbolically bringing forth the development of a remarkable vision. Just then, Coosewoon said "a big bird down at the creek" called to him, telling him to "walk down to the stream's edge." The unidentified bird addressed Kenneth directly and the Comanche followed the instructions, walking the short distance down to the banks of Sallisaw Creek. At the time, Kenneth did not understand what was taking place "but I knew it was spiritual." All the time, Coosewoon kept wondering what all this was about, all the while holding onto the blue ember. "So I had that glowing wooden chip in my hand and as I walked down to where that bird was calling me, that ember started getting brighter and brighter." Although confused but not scared by these happenings, Coosewoon "believed it was something truly spiritual." Since Kenneth believed in spiritual experiences and had seen and heard the Great Spirit in the hospital, he was somewhat prepared for the Great Vision.

Coosewoon began to pray to himself while he stood on the creek bank, pondering the events before him. All of a sudden, a strong wind started blowing up to his left where he could see an open prairie. "A big gust of wind," blew through the woods where Kenneth stood holding the blue ember, and soon the wind "went right through me and by me." Kenneth looked up "into the sky and saw lightning." He heard the roar of thunder. It began to rain slightly, although when Kenneth looked up, he saw no clouds and believed it was raining just in that small spot where he stood. He felt as if he was in the middle of the universe, with one sky above and the earth below. He peered out in the various directions and finally saw some flash and zigzag lightning. The entire scene was just "like a movie" and Kenneth was in the middle of a real life drama. By this time, Coosewoon admitted he was "getting scared" but he simply did not understand the meaning of these dramatic events.

Kenneth began asking himself, "what is all this about?" Then the drama turned to another field of activity as a large oak tree in front of him "started dancing and shaking." In fact, Kenneth felt "an earthquake all around him as the whole earth shook." The earth shook and trees danced, bouncing him "about ten feet in the air." All this activity made Coosewoon question more and more the meaning of these dramatic events, when even more events unfolded.

All of a sudden, he saw two lights coming through the woods beyond the creek and thought people might be walking through the forest in from of him with two flashlights, but the lights came to the far side of the creek and Kenneth could clearly see that no one held torches of any sort. The lights had a life of their own and appeared in the black night "like two eyes that blinked." The light swirled into a ball of blue light, glowing and rolling in the darkness. It moved across Sallisaw Creek, diffusing into a blue glowing fog that crossed the stream and surrounded Kenneth about waist high. "It circled me, that blue glow," Kenneth recalled. "I tried to reach and get some of it" so "I reached down and touched it to find out what it was." As he tried to capture and feel the blue foggy light, a voice called out to him, saying:

"No, don't touch me!" So Kenneth raised his hand away from the glowing blue light, all the while holding the blue ember in his other hand.

Immediately after withdrawing his hand, the blue light surrounding his body seemed to speak to Kenneth, saying, "I want you to run Sweat Lodge Ceremonies." The spiritual voice seemed to be a male and spoke to Kenneth as if coming from the blue foggy light. "You run the sweats," the Spirit said, "and I'll show you how to run them. I will teach you everything you need to know and I'll always be with you. I'll never leave you." The Spirit promised, "you will see many miracles and many good things will happen." The Spirit urged Kenneth to trust in Him and He "promised always to help me with the Sweat Lodge," provided "I would help others." Speaking out loud, Coosewoon said, "I'm no leader of the Sweat Lodge" and "I don't have anything to run the sweats with." The Grandfather heard Kenneth and answered, saying, "get a water bucket and a dipper." Kenneth understood the meaning of these instructions since the leader of the Sweat Lodge used a bucket and dipper to pour water onto the glowing hot rocks inside the Sweat Lodge. According to Kenneth, the Grandfather then said: "Start with that," meaning the water bucket and dipper.

Just as quickly as these events began to occur, they ended. The woods turned silent, except for the sound of the crackling fire. Coosewoon looked into his hand to see if the blue ember was still there. He found it still warm within his hand and he saw the chip of wood still appearing blue. He put the chip into his pocket and returned to the fire to add more wood while he contemplated the events that had so recently swirled around him. He wondered about the meaning of the messages given to him but he had no interest

81

in leading the Sweat Lodge Ceremony or healing others. That was not what he was about.

When the men returned from Dwight Mission, they continued the Sweat Lodge Ceremony they had started earlier. Kenneth said nothing to the men about what he had experienced. In fact, it was some time before he told anyone about the Great Vision or the Blue Medicine that he had seen glow blue, or the chip he had held in his hand. Little did he know it at the time, but the Blue Medicine he held in his hand would be a gift from the Grandfather, a portion of his medicine that he would give to patients to ingest orally into their body as part of the healing process. Throughout his Great Vision, Coosewoon held the Blue Medicine in his hand. He did not know it at the time, but this element of nature, a gift of the Grandfather, would become an element of his medicine to help heal others. But at the time he received these medicine gifts, Coosewoon had no idea of the power given him. He would learn this through personal experience in due time when the Grandfather led Kenneth into the Sweat Lodge Ceremony.

Kenneth's experiences at Dwight Mission proved remarkable, as he had several spiritual experiences inside and outside of the lodge that changed his life forever. These moving events changed his life in amazing ways and remain critical to his life and teachings today. His place within the shamanistic world of contemporary America stems from his visionary experiences in the hospital and at Dwight Mission. Kenneth Coosewoon used the spiritual knowledge gained during the Great Vision to start a new life as a holy man, committed to helping others. Not long after the Great Vision, he would begin his work as a Native American healer, drawing on his own experiences and the gifts provided to him by the Grandfather, and the songs and advice of his friends, Wallace and Gracie Black Elk.

Significance of the Black Elks

For many years, Wallace and Gracie Black Elk had traveled together to bring the Sweat Lodge to people of all races and to lecture to many diverse groups about medicine ways of their Lakota people. On two occasions, these two Lakota elders lectured at San Diego State University, addressing students studying American Indian Studies. Like Coosewoon, they shared their wisdom and cultural ways with Native American and non-Native students. The Black Elks did not discriminate about sharing their spiritual traditions, often lecturing to mixed groups and offering healing to anyone that asked for help. They never charged people to participate in ceremony or turned away people who were not of Native heritage. They helped all people, including Kenneth Coosewoon. Native Americans became the primary participants in ceremonies led by the Black Elks, but they helped everyone, regardless of their age, gender, race, or ailment.

Wallace and Gracie had been asked to lead the workshop at Dwight Mission, and Coosewoon attended the gathering not knowing a great deal about the Black Elks or the Sweat Lodge Ceremony. This was Kenneth's first of many meetings with the Black Elks who became personal friends, confidents, and teachers. Some time later, when Kenneth began conducting the Sweat Lodge Ceremony, the words spoken by the Grandfather through the blue swirling light began to make sense. The Grandfather promised always to walk with Coosewoon and help him. According to Kenneth, the Grandfather reassured him that all things he needed to do the work would come to him. Promises made were fulfilled with time and patience but realized, and Kenneth witnessed many miracles.

In addition, the Grandfather had promised to provide all things necessary for Kenneth to do his healings. Over time, people gave Kenneth many things, including eagle feathers, a drum, songs, pipe, an eagle bone whistle, cedar, sage, and other sacred items. But "when I first started, " Kenneth explained, "I had a dipper and water bucket." Other things all came to him with time, and in this way, he learned patience and trust in the Grandfather. Kenneth explained, "in life we want something right now, but He doesn't do it that way. When He's ready for you to have the next step, He will provide it." Coosewoon remained skeptical of the healing spirit and the messages he had received, but Kenneth remembered the voice saying, "son, don't worry about it! Whenever anything good happens, don't worry about it." Coosewoon learned to "put a smile on your face and keep going."

Learning the Sweat Lodge Ceremony

As Coosewoon grew into his role as a healer, he learned to conduct Sweat Lodge Ceremonies. This took place over a period of time, using methods he used from the Southern and Northern Plains. Most of all, Coosewoon would explain he learned how to do ceremony and heal others by listening to the teachings of the Grandfather. As a result, Kenneth performs his own method of Sweat Lodge, using elements common among the Comanche, Kiowa, Arapaho, Cheyenne, and Lakota. Indian tribes throughout the

Native Universe perform Sweat Lodge Ceremony in several diverse ways. Coosewoon explains, "there's no one way to do the Sweat Lodge; they are all good ways of bringing the Grandfather into close contact with people who need His help."

Kenneth listened and learned from Wallace and Gracie Black Elk, but his central teachings came from the Creator or the Great Holy One that brings the healing light and spirit into the Sweat Lodge. Coosewoon explained the Grandfather had introduced the Sweat Lodge to indigenous people at the beginning of time. Often, the creation songs and stories of various Native people contain the origin account of how the Sweat Lodge came to the people or how it was first used.

Coosewoon explained, "I'm Comanche and Kiowa, but I don't run the sweat in any tribally specific manner, just the way I grew into the ceremony." Kenneth felt from the beginning that the Sweat Lodge Ceremony was about health and healing, not the specific format of the ceremony. "We are all different tribes . . . and the ceremony means the same to all Native Americans that practice the Sweat Lodge." Coosewoon believed that "it's not bad" for tribal healers to follow their tribe's traditions in conducting the Sweat Lodge. In fact, Kenneth felt that it was natural for healers to do so, but Coosewoon employed the ways he learned from the Healing Spirit or the Grandfather and other Native American healers he trusted.

In like fashion, he learned his Sweat Lodge songs from Gracie Black Elk who made a gift of her songs to Coosewoon telling him that one day he would use them to help others. According to Coosewoon, when he speaks to a group about Gracie Black Elk or at times in the Sweat Lodge, she appears to him in spirit. Kenneth reported that "Gracie appears to me in the Sweat Lodge Ceremony singing along with the group" as Coosewoon conducts healings.

Since that first experience in the Cookson Hills, Kenneth has devoted his life to helping others. Before her untimely death of a heart attack in 1999, Doraline, his first wife, joined Coosewoon in the work along with Rita Barnhardt, Kenneth's second cousin. He knew Rita from Elgin High School and Rita worked for Kenneth as a cook when he managed the Drop-In Center. The three traveled together working to heal and help prisoners, veterans and children. Kenneth and Rita continued that work after Doraline's death and later they married.

Early on, as Kenneth began leading the Sweat Lodge, he decided that he should try to include both men and women in the Sweat Lodge Ceremony, "so the power and healing comes in much stronger." Coosewoon believes, "you see, you need both a man and woman to complete the power in the best way and I like to have both men and women come into the sweat so I can better help others. It brings in the healing to that place." Over time, Kenneth added Beverly Patchell as a female assistant. He and a female helper worked as a healing team through the Sweat Lodge. Any person, regardless of their background, race, or circumstance may ask Kenneth, Rita or Beverly for help. They respond by offering their healing methods to anyone who is sincere in their request.

When Kenneth and Rita take people into the Sweat Lodge for healing, they can never predict the results of a ceremony. They can never predict the consequence of healing ceremony. Whether a person receives healing or not, is up to the Grandfather, not humans. Coosewoon explained that he never knows what images, characters, or forms might join them in their ceremony, but he believes strongly that the Sweat Lodge, songs, and prayers act as a conduit to the spirit world that may bring healing to participants. The Grandfather decides who will be healed, not Kenneth or his assistants.

According to Coosewoon, during the Sweat Lodge Ceremony, "everyone doesn't see the same thing." During a Sweat Lodge Ceremony, a multitude of images, visitations, sounds, songs, and feelings may appear. "If you're spiritually ready, you're going to see a lot of different signs, different things in there, but if you're not ready, you won't." He felt that by promising never to drink again, joining Alcoholics Anonymous, working at the alcohol treatment center, building the Sweat Lodge on Cache Creek, and participating in his first Sweat Lodge Ceremony with his clients in Lawton, he had prepared himself for the spiritual messages that came to him. However, given the many times Kenneth unsuccessfully attempted to commit suicide and failed, as well as the messages the Grandfather gave Coosewoon while he was in the hospital, it appears the spiritual world always had larger and more long-term plans for Coosewoon to help others. However, Coosewoon first had to help himself first by abstaining from alcohol.

Kenneth followed the Grandfather's instructions and stopped drinking. Since his days in the hospital, Coosewoon's life has unfolded in a positive and spiritual manner that encouraged him to seek greater cultural understanding and follow his own Indian identity. Kenneth's work in alcohol and drug prevention and treatment led him to the Sweat Lodge, and his Great Vision brought him face to face with the Grandfather through fire, wood, light, sound, song, wind, and spiritual voices that spoke directly to him, instructing him to lead the Sweat Lodge.

During the remainder of his time at Dwight Mission, Kenneth contemplated the messages he had received but he told no one of the events. When he returned home to Medicine Park, Coosewoon told no one about his experiences. He did not tell Doraline or his children or his friends. He worried that people would say he was hallucinating and his visions could not be true. Kenneth attempted to understand the meaning of the things he had witnessed at Dwight Mission and make sense of it all. The words spoken by the voice emanating from the blue light kept rolling round in his head. "Imagine, the Grandfather wanted me to lead the Sweat Lodge!" Over and over he thought about the request or instruction that he should run the Sweat Lodge Ceremony and help others. Again and again, Kenneth wondered why he would be asked to conduct a ceremony he barely knew. He kept thinking about the promise, "I will always be with you." The Great Vision fit neatly into the motif of ancient songs and stories among indigenous people, with the Creator taking many forms and teaching people the mysteries of life.

With time, the events surrounding the vision became more clearly defined to Coosewoon, but he still did not know the full significance of the messages. Kenneth's views about his own place on earth changed over time and his personal understanding of his life evolved in his heart, mind, and soul through experiences, and prayers. Knowledge about how he was to lead the Sweat Lodge came with time and unusual experiences that continued the magical events he first experienced in the Indian hospital in Lawton. Only later did he feel that spirits had appeared to him at Dwight Mission to cleanse his heart, mind, and spirit. In fact, during the ceremony in the Cookson Hills, Kenneth saw blood shooting in periodic spurts from his chest, and the rawhide rattle sang a medicine song that helped purify his body, blood, mind, and soul. Years later, Kenneth explained, "that rattle was like a blessing to me. It kept going around me in the dark and I thought someone held it in his hand but no one was there. It moved all around me in the air." The spiritual experience cleared Coosewoon's mind and the light purged his heart of the anger, anxiety, hatred, insecurity, ego, and resentment. For many years, he had carried these and other psychological baggage in his heart and mind. Kenneth's bleeding heart, animated by a beam of light from the hot rocks, symbolized a continuance of a personal healing process, which ultimately led him into the Sweat Lodge Ceremony.

Healing Jaime through Sweat Lodge

Not long after returning home to southwestern Oklahoma, Kenneth's daughter, Deanna, called him in a frantic tone, asking for his help. Deanna told her father that her boyfriend, Jaime, had been shot point blank with a .38 pistol. During the course of an armed robbery, an outlaw had shot Jaime in the stomach, exploding his liver and bringing the young man to the brink of death. The day after an unknown gunman shot Jaime, Deanna called her Dad to say that Jaime was in the hospital fighting for his life, and he needed help. When Deanna called, she asked Kenneth to come to the hospital. Although Kenneth liked Jaime a great deal, he did not want to join his family and Deanna at the hospital. "I figured they'd all be crying and fussing, and I did not want to get in the middle of that gathering." He asked Deanna, "well what can I do?" His daughter asked

him to come to the hospital to be with her. She needed
Kenneth's support, so she asked him to help her. Reluctantly,
Coosewoon agreed to go to the hospital in Lawton, because
he wanted to be supportive of Deanna.

Before joining Deanna at the hospital and paying
a short visit to Jaime, Kenneth cleaned up. He shaved and
took a shower, all the time thinking of Jaime's condition. As
he showered, "A big jolt went through me, like an electrical
shock. It hit me hard. And then I heard the voice return
to me, very clear." Coosewoon heard the same voice that
he had heard at Dwight Mission. Kenneth remembers the
voice saying: "Kenneth, you do not know the power of the
medicine I have given you. Go use it on Jaime." The voice
was clear and direct. Today, Coosewoon would say, "the
voice I heard was that of the Grandfather, although at the
time, I didn't know it." While he showered, Coosewoon kept
thinking of the voice and its message: "Kenneth, you do not
know the power I have given you. Now go use it and help
Jaime." Coosewoon understood that this was a spiritual
message, but he did not know initially what he could do
to help Jaime. But back at Dwight Mission, the Spirit voice
had said, "I will always be with you and all things will come
to you." So Kenneth trusted in the Spirit and drove to the
hospital, not knowing how he might help Jaime. Kenneth
visited Jaime for the first time and the message came to him
through the "voice" that he should do Sweat Lodge Ceremony
for Jaime.

At the hospital, Coosewoon learned that Jaime was in
very bad shape. In fact, medical doctors did not expect him
to live. His condition was critical and life threatening due to
the abdominal wound and catastrophic injury to the liver.
Kenneth knew Jaime was unconscious, but he prayed for the

life of the young man. Kenneth had never led a Sweat Lodge Ceremony but he wanted Jaime to live, and he believed the Grandfather would help him in the ceremony. Kenneth got on the telephone and called the Kiowa, Cheyenne, Arapaho, and other Native American clients from the treatment center. He asked them to meet him at the Sweat Lodge on Cache Creek. Kenneth's grandson Ronald Cooper joined the men to assist in the healing ceremony. Coosewoon contacted the men who had been a part of the treatment program at the old Fort Sill Indian School. These men had first introduced Kenneth to Sweat Lodge and had built a Sweat Lodge down by Cache Creek adjacent to the school.

Kenneth drove to the Fort Sill Boarding School. As he approached the Sweat Lodge down by the creek, he witnessed a marvelous sight. According to Coosewoon, "when we got to the Sweat Lodge, hundreds of birds were circling. We saw eagles and hawks, robins and crows. There were lots of sparrows and blackbirds, every kind of bird, big and small." Kenneth was not sure what this meant, but "I took it as a good sign." The good sign seemed to favor a positive Sweat Lodge Ceremony. Coosewoon and some of the men built a fire and began to heat the rocks, while others made prayer ties and began to prepare for the ceremony.

When Coosewoon and his clients entered the darkness of the Sweat Lodge with no light except those emanating from the hot rocks, Kenneth spoke from his heart to his clients in a humble manner. He told them the story about Jaime's ill-fated gunshot wound and the fact that he was near to death. He told his clients he needed their collective prayers for healing. "All of you know me," Coosewoon announced. "I don't know a lot about the Sweat Lodge but I do know that our collective prayer for Jaime will be stronger than just my prayer." So he asked the men to pray for Coosewoon's guidance and Jaime's healing as he led the ceremony. Kenneth then asked everyone to pray for Jaime's life. They prayed four rounds, going in and out of the Sweat Lodge a total of four times, the sacred number of many Native Americans. After the sweat, Kenneth "felt good about the ceremony." Ronald remembered that upon leaving the Sweat Lodge the opposite side of Cache Creek glowed a florescent blue. This was seen as a good sign.   Kenneth returned to the hospital to check on Jaime.

Jaime was a Catholic, and hospital officials had called in a priest to give Jaime his last rites. Kenneth watched as the priest read over Jaime and spread holy water on the young man. In his head, Kenneth clearly heard the voice again, saying that Jaime would not die. Kenneth had received this message during the Sweat Lodge Ceremony, and he was anxious to tell Jaime not to worry because he would live through this terrible experience. Kenneth reported that he heard the voice tell him to inform Jaime that he should hang on as he was going to make it. "Jaime will live!" When the priest left, Kenneth bent over Jaime and whispered into his ear. "Don't give up, Jaime. You're going to make it. We're going to do Sweat Lodge for you." Although unconscious, Kenneth detected a slight smile on Jaime's face and he briefly opened his eyes, messages that the young man had heard Coosewoon and would fight to live.

When Kenneth returned to the hospital the next day, he noticed a large horned owl outside the hospital. Among many Native American tribes, the owl is a messenger or sign of death. Coosewoon knew this and did "battle with the owl, telling him he would not win Jaime's life." He talked to the owl and told him to leave the hospital area. Kenneth told the owl that Jaime was going to live. "In a way, I did battle with that owl [death], but in the end, he knew I would win and Jaime would live."

Kenneth learned from the doctors that Jaime had stabilized but was still in critical condition. The doctors explained they had cobbled together portions of Jaime's liver and placed it into a plastic bag or container. The .38 caliber bullet had blown Jaime's liver to pieces, and the doctors tried to put the pieces together into a working organ. The medical staff had placed Jaime's blood vessels into the mass of liver pieces, collectively held together in a "plastic bag," but they could not get his blood to start flowing through the reconstructed liver. The doctors told Kenneth they believed they would be able to fly Jaime to the University of Oklahoma Medical Center in Oklahoma City, provided they could get his blood flowing through his liver. Kenneth learned that if the doctors in Lawton could stabilize Jaime, he might have a chance to get to Oklahoma City and live. Coosewoon decided that he needed to conduct another Sweat Lodge Ceremony.

"So I called my clients, the men that had done the first Sweat Lodge and we did it again," Coosewoon related. The group met again to heat up the sacred rocks, and they took the rocks to the center of the lodge, the heart of the "little church." There they prayed long and hard for the blood to start flowing through the pieces of liver bound up in the plastic container. Kenneth led his second ceremony for the benefit of Jaime. Coosewoon and his clients collectively asked the Grandfather to intervene for Jaime and allow the blood vessels to begin working. They prayed four rounds in the lodge, asking Grandfather to circulate the blood through Jaime's liver, Jaime's only chance to live. So Coosewoon and the men prayed for Jaime's blood to circulate in the man-made container of his pieces of liver. They prayed hard that Jaime might stabilize sufficiently to allow the medical staff to fly him by helicopter to Oklahoma City. At the University of Oklahoma Medical Center, they hoped specialists could take over and save Jaime.

After Coosewoon and his friends prayed for Jaime's blood to begin circulating, Kenneth returned to the hospital. There he learned that Jaime's blood had started to circulate, and it appeared as if his liver was beginning to cleanse the blood. Sometime during Jaime's ordeal, Kenneth gave Jaime some of his Blue Medicine to swallow and "it seemed to help." Coosewoon had a premonition that the bark he had held through the blue ember has healing power, and he used it to

Not far from the Fort Sill Indian School, Kenneth Coosewoon and his clients conducted Sweat Lodge Ceremonies along Cache Creek. In the woods to the left in this photograph on the far side of the creek bank, Coosewoon helped build the lodge where he experienced his first ceremony. It was here that Kenneth, Ronald Cooper, and various clients prayed for Jaime's recovery after being shot.

help Jaime and others after Jaime's ordeal. Kenneth and the others met again and again to ask the Grandfather to stabilize Jaime sufficiently so he could be transferred. They prayed, each time with Kenneth leading the ceremony and praying for healing. Coosewoon often explains that "prayers are the most powerful things on earth," and in this case, Kenneth claimed that the Grandfather answered the prayers.

Jaime improved. His blood continued to flow through the liver and he grew sufficiently better so that a medical air ambulance took him to the University Medical Center where specialists used the most recent discoveries in medical science to save his life. Doctors and nurses in Oklahoma City gave Jaime life-saving care. At first, Jaime improved at the medical center but then he had a turn for the worse because of gangrene infection within the liver. Jaime called Kenneth asking him what he should do, and Coosewoon advised the young man to do what the doctors recommended. They were the experts.

But gangrene developed rapidly and thoroughly in Jaime's liver. Kenneth called his clients again and asked them to meet him at the Sweat Lodge. Once he had his clients together, he told them of the ugly infection inside of Jaime's liver. By this time, the men helping Coosewoon understood the severity of Jaime's condition and they understood the consequences of gangrene setting into the internal wound. Together they prayed and prayed hard that the Grandfather would remove the infection. According to Kenneth, at the very time the men met to pray in the Sweat Lodge, the infection started to break up and the drain from Jaime's liver started flowing a great deal of infection. In fact, during that time period, Jaime's body drained three bags of gangrene. The next day, Kenneth learned that all of the infection had left

Jaime's body and he had no more gangrene inside the liver or any other spot in his body. Jaime started to gain strength and his liver began working perfectly. He was on the road to recovery.

Jaime lived through the experience and remains alive today, ready and able to confirm this story and verify its contents. Coosewoon's association with the Sweat Lodge Ceremony grew greatly after leading his first ceremonies. His life changed dramatically as a result of Jaime's tragedy and healing, providing a platform for Kenneth to begin his life leading the Sweat Lodge and healing people in need. Through the entire experience, Kenneth learned to lead the Sweat Lodge, and he believed strongly the Grandfather had given him the gift of healing.

Leading the Sweat Lodge

Since leading his first Sweat Lodge Ceremonies, Kenneth Coosewoon has led thousands of ceremonies and helped thousands of people. He described his method of conducting the ceremony, and explained he learned from the Grandfather, his clients, the Black Elks, and others. He follows no prescribed format and allows each ceremony to unfold in an original, organic manner. Still, he follows a basic outline that he shared with me during several interviews.

Before the sweat, Kenneth begins the ceremony in prayer, wrapping several tobacco prayer ties and praying for others, particularly participants who will join him in the Sweat Lodge. He makes prayer wraps numbering five to seven small strands of bundles, depending "on the strength of the prayer needed." Kenneth explains, "you can use five but seven is better." He adds, "you can use seven if it is a serious emergency" or "if it is heavy duty stuff, otherwise, you can just use five."

During most ceremonies, Coosewoon places prayer ties on the ribs of the Sweat Lodge. He uses the prayer ties in a special way in the Sweat Lodge. "You don't tie the string of prayer ties to the ribs, you just push them up into the ribs of the lodge." At the same time Coosewoon uses prayer ties, he generally uses cedar as part of the ceremony. "A lot of the time when you take a prayer tie, you use cedar too." A patient or participant might give it to Kenneth, and "I'll take it out to a far area and we'll burn it." He uses the cedar as a prayer to send smoke "that goes up to the Grandfather who will answer your prayers." Coosewoon explains that a person does not "have to reveal what you put on the prayer tie," which means that the person making the prayer tie asks for specific help through a prayer when placing the tobacco into the red cloth and wrapping it with string.

Even before Kenneth constructs the Sweat Lodge, he gathers the proper rocks necessary to conduct the ceremony. Coosewoon gathers his rocks from a special place not far from his home. Coosewoon seeks most of the rocks used in his Sweat Lodge on Mount Scott in the heart of Comanche and Kiowa country. Kenneth and Rita Coosewoon gather rocks together, praying before they take the rocks and explaining to the rocks that they are removing them from their place on earth to be used in the Sweat Lodge Ceremony intended to help others. They pray to the Grandfather, thanking him for the rocks and blessing those that will benefit from their healing heat. These rocks, Kenneth explained, "hold the heat good. The rocks are heavy and round. Everything we use in the Sweat Lodge is round."

When Kenneth tends to the rocks, he builds a large fire around them with thick, heavy wood approximately four feet tall and six inches thick. He heats them until they are glowing red-hot. When he heats the rocks in this way, Coosewoon feels he brings new life to the ancient rocks, returning the essence of the rocks back to the creation when natural conditions created them with intense heat. Coosewoon or the "rock boy" places the large round rocks in the center of the Sweat Lodge where Kenneth ultimately pours water over them, creating a great deal of steam that fills the sacred space. The "steam is like the Grandfather, it penetrates and goes through you, cleaning you, healing you, purifying you." The Sweat Lodge "cleans you" both physically and spiritually, provided those participating keep an honest and open heart and mind about the ceremony.

Within the Sweat Lodge, the rocks form the center of the ceremonial lodge. Extremely hot rocks are used to heat the lodge and emit heat and steam to cleanse the mind, body, and soul. The Sweat Lodge is always a holy place, even when the ceremony is not occurring. Kenneth once explained that he sometimes enters the lodge just to be in the spiritual space where he feels close to the Grandfather and can pray. During ceremony, the Sweat Lodge becomes another form of holy place, a sacred space for multiple people seeking help and healing. Kenneth asks all participants to enter the lodge with an open mind and in a positive state of mind. In this way, he can summon the Healing Spirit to enter the lodge and help those in need.

Once participants are in the Sweat Lodge and prepared for ceremony, Kenneth opens the ceremony with song and prayer. Kenneth begins every ceremony in this manner, offering an opening prayer. In his own words, he once shared the following with me: "I'll say a prayer and sing a song," which calls out to the Grandfather Spirit in poetic form:

> Great Spirit, Great Spirit
> Have pity on us
> Having a hard time
> We need your help
> We need you!

Black Elk and his wife, Gracie, had taught Kenneth this song, giving it to him and urging him to use it to open each ceremony. After the opening song and prayer, Kenneth asks participants in the Sweat Lodge to pray. If the person is self-conscious, he asks them to offer a silent prayer. Coosewoon explains that during his ceremonies, "if you don't want to pray out loud," in the Sweat Lodge, "you don't have to." Kenneth asks the person praying to end their prayer with the words, "All My Relations." This phrase, so common among Lakota, Dakota, and other Plains Indians, indicates the person has completed their prayer. Like Wallace Black Elk, Kenneth also uses this technique, because of his belief that all people are kin, children of the Grandfather.

While a person is praying, Coosewoon prays for that person, asking Grandfather to hear the prayers and help that specific person. He might place sage, cedar, tobacco, or other offerings on the hot rocks, asking prayers for the participant then praying for help. When Coosewoon runs a sweat, he encourages all participants to be positive in their approach to the Sweat Lodge Ceremony, which will benefit the individual and the community of participants in any particular sweat. He asks that as a group, participants place their minds in balance with positive act for all people, but particularly those people suffering from illnesses, drug and alcohol abuse, sexual abuse, excessive tobacco use, overeating, and mental illnesses.

Once the ceremony is underway, Coosewoon pours water on the hot rocks, which fills the dark space with steam. "I take the dipper and pour it over the rocks," Kenneth explained, "and it makes steam that goes all through our bodies." The steam is an element of the divine, the holy water that transforms into another form that cleans the body and soul, purifying the person. It causes healing for those in need. Coosewoon believes the steam offers a method by which the Creator moves within the Sweat Lodge and enters the bodies of all the participants. Kenneth stated that various "tribes have different ways of running their sweat, but I was told that when you go into the Sweat Lodge, you must enter with two things in mind. You enter the Sweat Lodge seeking help and healing from Grandfather, and you enter the ceremony with an open mind." According to Coosewoon, "as long as you go in for those two things, you'll never go wrong."

Like all healers, Coosewoon believes that it is essential for patients to believe in the efficacy of his medicine, and they must believe that inexplicable things can and do happen in and out of the Sweat Lodge. Indeed, Kenneth says that miracles happen in the Sweat Lodge Ceremony. He has witnessed many examples of men and women being cured of cancer, heart disease, alcoholism, liver disease, eye trouble, skin ailments, and back problems. Most important, he has witnessed healing of mental illnesses and severe depression that had plagued participants for years. Coosewoon never takes credit for the healing as he explains, "the healing is from the Grandfather, not me. I am working to bring to the medicine to the person but the Creator decides if that person will be healed or not. I cannot direct that."

Within the Sweat Lodge during ceremony, Kenneth is careful not to get the lodge too hot and make people uncomfortable. "I don't want the experience inside there to be uncomfortable for people. They will start thinking of the heat and not the reason we're in the Sweat Lodge." This is especially true when he invites children and elders to a Sweat Lodge Ceremony, where he does not want them to feel overheated and ill from the heat and steam.

For several years, for example, Kenneth has conducted the Sweat Lodge Ceremony in San Marcos, Texas, for the San Marcos Treatment Center. During different times of the year, but especially during Christmas and New Year's week, Kenneth spends over two weeks with young children enrolled in a school for the physically and mentally impaired. The children come from diverse cultures, but Kenneth feels that the children are some of the "smartest" and most "sensitive" children he has ever known. In 2011, one of the boys participating in the Sweat Lodge with Kenneth prayed that his mother would survive a cancer-related operation. The boy and group prayed for healing for the boy's mother. Approximately a month after the boy had prayed in the Sweat Lodge, he entered the holy space again with Coosewoon and thanked the Grandfather for healing his mother. Her cancer had disappeared and his mother did not have to undergo surgery. As long as Kenneth knew the boy, his mother remained cancer free.

During Coosewoon's Sweat Lodge Ceremonies at the San Marcos Treatment Center, he usually uses red berry cedar to cleanse the holy space of the Sweat Lodge. In fact, Kenneth often uses red berry cedar from his area to offer to the spirit world during the sweat. As people pray and at various times, Kenneth will place cedar on top of the hot rocks in the Sweat Lodge and say prayers, believing his prayers and those of participants will travel up to Grandfather in the sweet-smelling smoke the cedar creates. Since the Sweat Lodge is a re-creation of the universe, Kenneth proclaimed that the Grandfather comes into the lodge and dwells in that sacred space during ceremony. The Spirit may be seen in different forms, such as a mouse, eagle, wolf, or human form. Sometimes the Spirit is unseen, but the power permeates the Sweat Lodge and can enter those people seeking supplication. When the ceremony ends, a patient generally takes the prayer ties down from the ribs of the lodge to hang them in a house or car. In case of bedridden patients, Coosewoon places the prayer ties along the headboard of the patient's bed.

Kenneth has pointed out often that all human beings are related. He explains, "we're all kin to all of God's creation. Everything that God created is kin too, and that's why we say, 'All My Relations.'" Kenneth has adapted the Lakota phrase for his Sweat Lodge, believing strongly that all human beings are truly related, regardless of their race, ethnicity, or culture. He feels that Native Americans are brothers and sisters to each other, and as human beings, American Indians are related to all other people and have something to offer to the world—a united belief in humanity's connection with each other, and with all of Creation on earth and the universe. Having knowledge of this is a contribution of Native America to the world. It is certainly a transnational concept and one that has guided traditional Native Americans for generations.

Throughout a sweat, Kenneth prays continually, asking for healing whatever ails the people in attendance. He asks participants to turn everything over to the Grandfather, especially those things beyond human control. Coosewoon recognizes that human beings are limited in their ability to effect their health and the outcomes of their lives or problems. He believes the Creator has a hand in human affairs and can be a positive influence, if approached correctly and in a spiritual manner. He emphasized that the Grandfather controls the people participating in ceremony and the outcome of their prayers. He urges people to humble themselves, and Kenneth humbles himself, asking the Grandfather for health, assistance, and positive outcomes that will benefit participants or their loved ones, the objects of the requests made by participants.

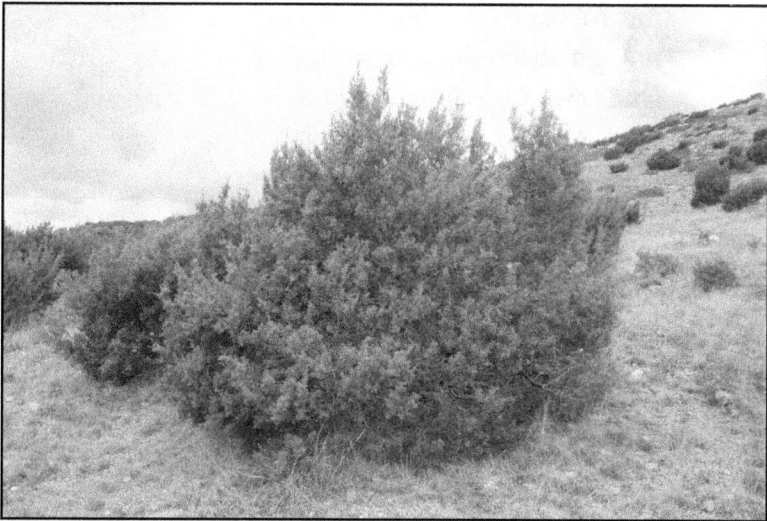

On April 12, 2015, Kenneth Coosewoon led a gathering party to Longhorn Mountain west of his home to cut the ends of the red berry cedar growing on the sides of the mountain. Coosewoon's mother used to tell him that Native American shamans and holy people traveled to this mountain from great distances to gather the unique and sacred ends of the cedar tree to use in ceremonies. Kenneth gathers cedar from this site to place on the hot rocks inside the Sweat lodge.

Concluding the Sweat

At the conclusion of the Sweat Lodge Ceremony, Coosewoon offers a closing prayer, often offering the words below:

> Our Bodies
> Our Prayers
> Out Hearts
> And Everything Sacred
> Release Our Hearts, Grandfather
> We give our lives over to you, Grandfather
> You can do everything in a good way, Grandfather
> Many things are beyond our control, Grandfather
> You are the Controller, Grandfather
> You can do anything, Grandfather
> That is why we come to you
> We ask you for help, Grandfather
> We ask you for health, Grandfather
> Bless these people, Grandfather

Coosewoon concludes the ceremony by pouring water over the hot rocks, saying, "water is holy" and asking the steam to enter the hearts, bodies, and minds of the participants. He also asks the steam, a manifestation of Grandfather, to bring health and healing to everyone. "Come over and penetrate our loved ones that are sick," Coosewoon asks in a prayer, a song of supplication. "Grandfather, help us and help them as this water goes through our bodies." He asks that the water take away all impurities of mind, spirit, and body. With that, the ceremony concludes.

Blue Medicine

One of the singular most important elements of the Great Vision proved to be the gift of the Blue Medicine. So many aspects of the vision appeared in the color blue and since that event, Kenneth has experienced the glowing blue color many times in the Sweat Lodge and in things he sees outside of the sweat. Blue is the color of the Spirit, and it is a common color associated with those things associated with the divine. When the sparks jumped out of the fire during his Great Vision, the voice of the Spirit spoke to Kenneth, telling him to pick up the blue ember. He gathered up the ember in his hand and held it throughout the vision. At the conclusion of the vision, the wood material in his hand glowed blue and became his medicine. Since the vision, Kenneth has used the Blue Medicine to help cure people, telling them to eat tiny portions of the wood. When Kenneth feels it is appropriate, he shares his Blue Medicine with patients and participants in the Sweat Lodge, especially people with special needs.

Coosewoon is convinced that "the wood has some spiritual effect to it, some way, but I don't know how." As a result of the efficacy of the Blue Medicine, Kenneth once contemplated having it analyzed by a chemist. Wallace Black Elk counseled him not to do this but to accept the power given the Blue Medicine by the Grandfather. Over time, Kenneth has accepted the power of items given to him by the Grandfather and learned simply to trust in the Creator, the great maker of Indian medicine. He believes that the Grandfather infused the Blue Medicine with healing agencies, just as he has placed such spiritual power in wood, water, flowers, leaves, seeds, sage, cedar, sweetgrass, pipe, feathers, bundles, tobacco, and other natural items. Kenneth sometimes creates leather medicine bundles that can include his medicine, sage, cedar, tobacco, and other items, urging patients to wear the bundles or keep them close to their bodies. He puts these bundles together through acts of prayer, and he finds them useful in treating others.

For people with cancer, heart disease, mental problems, abuse concerns, liver issues, headaches, spinal injuries, diseases, etc., he will use the Blue Medicine, breaking off a small piece of the wood and giving it to the person to eat. Kenneth commented, "lots of times when they're sick, I let them eat a little piece of that wood, which I combine with prayers and the eagle feather." The Blue Medicine has "some spiritual effect," that has a healing quality for some people. Sometime the medicine and Sweat Lodge Ceremony heals the person completely, and sometimes it only helps the person cope better with their illness. Coosewoon explained this phenomenon, saying, "it is not up to me whether the person is healed. The Grandfather decides what will result from our interaction in and out of the Sweat Lodge." In either case, if the patient believes in the Grandfather's power and efficacy of the Blue Medicine, the medicine works to aid the person.

In retrospect, Kenneth realized that the color blue that emerges as a continual theme during the Great Vision would play a highly significant role in his medicine way and ability to heal. A holy message came to him after seeing a blue charcoal glowing near the fire and a magnificent ball of blue light across the creek. The blue light diffused and became a fluorescent fog that glowed as it floated across the creek and surrounded Kenneth's body. During Coosewoon's vision experience at the Dwight Mission, the wood that appeared to Kenneth glowing blue became his medicine, infused with the power of the blue floating fog of blue light.

The Blue Medicine appears grey or tan to others, but Kenneth sees it in blue, and he has patients place his medicine into their body as part of the healing process. Coosewoon put it succinctly, saying "It's like putting part of the Grandfather into their bodies."

Kenneth takes his Blue Medicine whenever he travels, placing it in a small cedar chest to keep it with sage and his eagle feathers. "The wood is blue when I find it," Kenneth explained, and it glows blue in his eyes. But others do not see the wood as blue. If Coosewoon conducts healing ceremonies and runs out of his Blue Medicine, he goes out by himself and prays to Grandfather for more, and the Creator sends it to him. When he is in a darkened area or outside at night, Kenneth sees the bark glowing blue on the ground and picks it up. For Coosewoon, the Blue Medicine is "the gift that was given to me." He says, "I know when I do some doctoring, a lot of times when they're sick, I let them eat a little piece of that wood and with prayers and the eagle feather, they get well. That wood has some spiritual power to it. In some way it has healing power, but I don't know what it is." Coosewoon has never had the blue wood analyzed by a chemist, and he never will. He has simply accepted the gift and used it to heal others, not questioning how it helps them, except that the Blue Medicine is infused with the healing power of the Spirit. Kenneth and Rita chose to accept the power of the Blue Medicine without questioning its healing properties. And this decision has remained with them as they have traveled thousands of miles around the United States doctoring many people for nearly forty years.

Sweat Lodge Among Native Americans

Native Americans often point out the Sweat Lodge is an ancient dwelling that is alive with Spirit. It is a place where people ask the Creator for assistance in dealing with many of life's issues, especially illnesses. Kenneth Coosewoon calls the Sweat Lodge "the world's first little church" where people can "enter the spiritual world and ask Grandfather for help no matter what the problems." Kenneth first heard about the Sweat Lodge when he was young, although he knew virtually nothing about the Sweat Lodge Ceremony until he was an adult and not from members of his family. Some of his boyhood neighbors had a Sweat Lodge in their back yards, but Kenneth had little interest in learning about the small covered lodges. But the Sweat Lodge had been a part of Native American cultures for generations, not just on the Great Plains but also across the Native Universe.

During the late nineteenth century and the establishment of the modern reservation system in the United States, Indian agents outlawed the use of the Sweat Lodge Ceremony, believing it to be subversive. As a result, Indians wishing to practice the Sweat Lodge had to "go underground." Indians living on reservations had to hide their use of the Sweat Lodge Ceremony and other ceremonies outlawed by federal agents. In order to conduct ceremony, Indian leaders conducting ceremony had to sequester themselves far from the agencies. Gracie and Wallace Black Elk told Coosewoon that years before, they too had to conduct ceremonies in private locations away from agencies and representatives of the United States to heal others.

The Black Elks and the Grandfather taught Coosewoon, "there's nothing in the Sweat Lodge we don't use, including spirituality, purification, healing, psychology, and counseling." As Coosewoon put it, "you name it, and it's in there." Kenneth has come to believe that every part of the Sweat Lodge Ceremony is tied to things holy, direct links to the Creator. Willows used to make the ribs of the lodge come from the earth, and rocks taken from deep within the earth provide heat, light, and steam for the lodge. Coosewoon says stones used in the ceremony represent the body of Mother Earth. When he applies water to the hot rocks, and the lodge fills with steam, Coosewoon claims the steam is the moist breath of the Creator, which permeates the holy space of the lodge and enters the bodies of those participating in ceremony. The Sweat Lodge offers a unique environment that represents the universe. The water transforms into steam, and steam fills the entire environment of the lodge, cleansing a person's mind, body, and soul. Kenneth explains that the ceremony provides physical, mental, spiritual, and emotional healing to everyone that enters the Sweat Lodge with an open mind.

Some people know of the Sweat Lodge through the writings of John Epes Brown. In 1953, Brown published *The Sacred Pipe: Black Elk's Account of the Seven Rites of the Oglala Sioux.* In this volume, Lakota holy man Black Elk provided many details about the Lakota way of Inipi or Sweat Lodge Ceremony. John Brown learned details of the ceremony from Lakota holy man Black Elk, the first notable Black Elk of the nineteenth and early twentieth centuries, not Coosewoon's mentors Wallace and Gracie Black Elk. Brown conveys elements of the ceremony based on Black Elk's experiences. Other versions of the Sweat Lodge Ceremony exist, and Coosewoon points out that each tribe has their own way of constructing the lodge and performing the rituals, prayers, and procedures necessary for the ceremony. However, the Sweat Lodge among all the tribes includes humbling oneself to the Creator Grandfather, giving thanks, and asking for help through songs and prayers. All of the ceremonies involve heated rocks, although Kenneth has explained that one may use the Sweat Lodge as holy space and site of prayer and supplication without conducting an entire ceremony with rocks and steam. "I sometimes go into the Sweat Lodge to pray," Kenneth explained, "asking the Grandfather to help heal someone in great need." Additionally, some tribes use only heat from the rocks in their Sweat Lodge without using water to create steam.

Heroes and Community

Old traditional oral stories of Comanche, Kiowa, and other Indians emphasized community heroes over individual attainment. The Sweat Lodge was and is a communal healing activity with a few people sharing the experience at any one time. Like the heroes of the ancient oral narratives and songs, people participating in Sweat Lodge helped one another fight addiction and bring about sobriety as a group effort, not just an individual effort. In large part, the success of the Sweat Lodge Ceremony among many diverse indigenous people lies with its simplicity and its communal nature. It involves a group ceremony intended to support or heal every member in attendance. The concept and philosophy of the Sweat Lodge Ceremony is tied to cultural complexities of individual tribes and healers. But in practice, the Sweat Lodge offers a holy space to sing, pray, and counsel others. People confront themselves and the Grandfather within the Sweat Lodge, humbling their egos to ask for divine intervention. The Sweat Lodge offers a miniature universe where a person can connect with many elements of the natural world sent as messengers from the Grandfather, Creator, Master of Life, or Almighty to communicate with the human in need. Healers like Kenneth Coosewoon call on the Grandfather for help, humbly presenting the needs of people and asking for healing and guidance.

On special occasions, Kenneth wears his hair in braids and dons his vest and choker. During his lectures on college campuses, he often wears his red ribbon shirt and braids his hair. He also wears one of his medicine bags that he often gives away to a person in need of healing.

For nearly forty years, Kenneth Coosewoon has helped people in many ways. He has offered prayers, ceremonies, counseling, and common-sense advice. He has helped people from all walks of life. Often people ask Kenneth for advice about their health issues, or others ask him to pray for their loved ones and friends. People of all backgrounds ask him for advice about troubled people, particularly those suffering from drug and alcohol abuse. Others send him letters or talk to him on the telephone, asking him to pray for a person the next time he enters the Sweat Lodge. Sometimes, Kenneth does not know the person about whom he is asked to pray or conduct ceremony, and when time permits, he asks for photographs of the person in need of assistance. Often he is unaware to what extent his healing ceremonies and prayers have helped or healed. "Unless they write me or give me a call, I often don't know if we did any good." But he does receive word from some patients that contact him and tell him if they are doing better. Since 1978, Kenneth has held healing ceremonies hundreds of times for thousands of people.

Work in Prisons

After Kenneth experienced the Great Vision and began using Blue Medicine, he received a special calling to help men and women incarcerated in the prison systems. At first, he concentrated his efforts on the prisons of Oklahoma, but as time transpired, Coosewoon came to feel he should help prisoners in other states. Initially invited into the prisons, prison officials had to approve Kenneth as a "minister" in order for him to meet inmates. During the 1970s, only spiritual leaders such as ministers, priests, or rabbis could bring their religious ceremonies into Oklahoma's prisons. So Kenneth became a "minister" and entered prisons to heal the spiritual, mental, and physical wounds of prisoners.

Coosewoon did not mind the designation, as he believed he was doing the work of the Grandfather. He was surprised that prison officials feared that the Sweat Lodge Ceremony was connected to the Native American Church and the Peyote Religion. "They are two different ways of ceremony," Kenneth explained, "but they did not know and they worried we were doing Peyote." To allay fears of Peyote use and generally about the Sweat Lodge Ceremony, Kenneth invited prison officials—including Christian ministers—into the Sweat Lodge. At first, prison officials wore gloves when they handled sage, sweetgrass, feathers, pipe, tobacco, and Blue Medicine. Coosewoon took the prison officials into the Sweat Lodge and shared ceremony with them. In this manner, he overcame their fears and won their support for a ceremony intended to help prisoners through their incarceration, developing new values about life inside prison and beyond of the walls of their imprisonment.

Kenneth worked with men and women prisoners in many different prisons, including minimum, medium, and maximum-security prisons. For several years, he conducted Sweat Lodge Ceremony at the maximum-security prison at McAllister, Oklahoma. Kenneth Coosewoon had a calling to take the Sweat Lodge into prisons, and he was the first Native American spiritual leader (or one of the first) to bring the ceremony into prisons in Oklahoma, a very noteworthy action that spawned a new trend in the prisons of the United States. Certainly he was an early advocate of using the Sweat Lodge Ceremony with prisoners to help them with their problems and help them establish a spiritual direction in their lives. Kenneth had many remarkable experiences dealing with prisoners, but he remembered one particular hardened and angry woman with a life sentence serving her time in the Mabel Bassett Correctional Center in McCloud, Oklahoma.

Prison officials would not allow Kenneth to conduct a full Sweat Lodge Ceremony with the female inmates at Mabel Bassett Prison, but he met with the women to speak to them, give advice, and pray for their well-being. Kenneth remembered a large, tough woman who would have nothing to do with him or the other inmates, all of whom feared this woman. "She really hated herself and hated others too," Coosewoon commented. Kenneth intuitively realized this woman was her own worst enemy, and because she hated herself, she could not love or care for others.

By the time Coosewoon visited the Mabel Bassett Correctional Center, he had developed a "sixth sense" about others, psychically knowing deep things about others, including this rough female prisoner. Kenneth identified her problem from the onset and prayed for this woman, asking the Grandfather to help her open her heart and mind to the healing. His prayer was answered. Coosewoon encouraged her to come into the Spirit of the Sweat Lodge, a way of thinking and praying. As a result of that experience, "I saw her transform into a good person open to caring about others."

According to Kenneth, this woman carried very negative power within her mind, soul, and body. Kenneth's prayers led this woman into the Spirit and she found healing. Coosewoon claimed he could physically see her change as the bad medicine left her body. This woman became the matriarch of all the women, taking care of them and helping other female prisoners through their prison days.

Feeling the Pain of Others

At Mabel Bassett Prison and in many other circumstances, Kenneth learned that he would take on the feelings of the people he doctored. He would feel physical, mental, and spiritual pain of the people in need. Coosewoon reports that when he doctors a person, he often "takes on the pain" of the ill person and temporarily sacrifices his mind and body to absorb the pain suffered by the patient. He explains that he actually feels what the patient feels while he is in the Sweat Lodge or near the patient. Often he feels "a lot of pain sometimes, not always, but sometimes you feel great when everything is going well." Other times, Kenneth feels "sickness or real sadness." Other times, he has a hard time breathing, especially if the patient has a respiratory ailment, and he finds it hard to get through an entire healing ceremony.

During one curing ceremony held outside the Sweat Lodge and within an enclosed area of a university building, Coosewoon was nearly struck down with the pain. Kenneth had taken three people in need of help into a quiet, secluded area of a building. Once he was there, he lit sweetgrass and used his eagle feather to smudge the patients, praying all the while for help and healing. He then asked each of the patients to eat a small piece of his medicine, concluding his prayer with additional prayers and smudging. He tapped every person on the shoulders, chest, and head with the eagle feather before concluding his prayer. Everyone thanked Kenneth and left the area, but Coosewoon held back, leaning against a brick way and attempting to catch his breath. "You'll have to help me," he explained. "Help me to a chair." Kenneth leaned on the assistant for help walking out of the intimate area and into the main lecture hall. He barely made it to a folding chair before he collapsed. "I'll be OK in a minute or two," he said, trying to catch his breath. After a few minutes, Coosewoon reported, "I don't know who got healed in there, but someone did or maybe all of them. I got hit hard from their sickness. I feel OK now, but something terrible went into me and I really fell down." One woman he had doctored witnessed her cancer go into remission. Another woman found that her damaged liver from alcoholism regenerated completely. She received a new liver and did not have to receive a liver replacement. Apparently, Coosewoon's healing prayer helped all of the people, and he took on their pain. Coosewoon explained, "I did not make this happen. The Grandfather does the healing and decides who will receive the healing. I'm just here to help the Grandfather enter into their bodies."

At one Sweat Lodge Ceremony conducted in Texas, Coosewoon felt the extreme pain of the patient. Kenneth had a hard time remaining in the lodge due to the deep feelings he experienced. A male nurse participated in the ceremony, and Coosewoon began feeling ill from taking on the patient's illness. The nurse took Kenneth's pulse and became frightened for Kenneth's well-being. The nurse could not find a pulse in Coosewoon's body, and he believed Kenneth was dying or dead. However, Kenneth gained some strength and slowly crawled out of the Sweat Lodge. Kenneth sat down so the nurse could check his vitals and explained to the nurse that during healings, he often feels the pain or accepts the condition being treated. Almost immediately after leaving the Sweat Lodge, Coosewoon's heartbeat and vitals returned to normal. Within a short time, he felt much better. The nurse told Coosewoon, "You didn't have no pulse, no heartbeat, no nothing." Kenneth explained that he took on the illness and pain of the patient, which brought about the slow heart beat and severe pain which had made Coosewoon very ill while he was in the Sweat Lodge.

Bad Medicine

In accordance with the belief system of many Native Americans, disease can develop from diverse causation, including the passing of bad medicine from one person to another. Kenneth believes negative energy can cause disease and death. Coosewoon has helped cure people that have been "touched" by the ill intent of others. Among many people of the world, a belief exists that a person may be able to put "bad medicine" on another individual. From that time of contamination, Kenneth has helped people rid themselves or loved ones of negative energy placed on them by other people, objects, or places.

Coosewoon pointed out that he grew up thinking that no one or object could place negative energy into another human being. In the past, Kenneth did not know that people and places could "put" or "shoot" evil energy onto others. But as Kenneth developed in Native American medicine, he said he came to know that other people, certain places, and objects on earth could convey negative power to people. This condition could make one extremely ill. Native American languages have words for the negative energy, the condition surrounding the use of "bad medicine," and names for those that use such negative medicine and touch others. But tribal people often use the English word of "witchcraft" to convey the idea. Kenneth's positive power is superior to the negative touch of ill-intended individuals. An example may illustrate the use of negative medicine placed on another person.

In 2011, a Seneca Indian woman reported that someone had placed bad medicine on her body, and she asked Kenneth to rid her of evil medicine. Another Native American, a man, had touched the Seneca woman while she attended a national conference. The woman believed she had felt the bad energy enter her body when he touched her. Almost immediately, she became ill after this encounter and she asked Kenneth to cleanse her body, mind, and spirit. During a gathering of Native Americans addressing different medicine ways, Coosewoon took the Seneca aside, smudged her, and exorcised the bad medicine. Kenneth explained that he drove the bad medicine from her body and cleansed her with sage, brushing the negative essence placed on her body with his eagle feather.

On another occasion, a Native American man asked Coosewoon to cleanse him from the negative power of another person. Kenneth prayed and smudged the Native man and gifted him a medicine bundle, urging the man, "'wear this medicine bag every time you are working with other Native Americans, because people are jealous of you and want you to fail. They have put bad medicine on you and they might put it back on you, so wear this bag or put it in your pocket to ward off the bad medicine." Coosewoon helped these two people restore their natural balance, ward off evil, and negative energy. In this way, both people returned to a positive or holy condition. Both people had greater awareness of the bad medicine that some people could place on them, and Coosewoon encouraged them both to wear their medicine bundles.

Over many years, Kenneth has treated several people influenced negatively by bad medicine. He reported that one of his most remarkable healings dealt with a group of Satan Worshipers that had followed the teachings of the Devil for many years. The leader of the group had decided to lead a new life away from Satan and negative influences of the world. The group asked Kenneth for help in delivering them from evil, and he agreed to lead them in the Sweat Lodge where he could cleanse them of negative influences and set them on a new path within the positive light of the Grandfather. Coosewoon agreed to do a ceremony for them, and during the Sweat Lodge, he touched each person with his eagle feather, asking the negative forces of Satan to leave them. He also asked the positive forces of the Grandfather to come into that person. During the ceremony, Kenneth reported the Grandfather told him that he could rid people of negative power placed on them by those that deal in evil, ill health, and death. As a result, Kenneth has worked with many people to exorcise them of evil and bad medicine.

Grandfather's Strength and Foresight

On a journey to Boston, Massachusetts, Kenneth addressed a conference about his work with drug and alcohol addicts. In typical fashion, this lecture began on a very personal level, explaining to the audience his own addiction to alcohol and his personal struggles with liquor. Coosewoon provided the audience an abbreviated version the Great Vision and how his experiences in the hospital and on Sallisaw and Cache creek took him on a new adventure to serve others. He briefly explained the use of the Sweat Lodge Ceremony in healing others, and provided a question and answer period. After his lecture, a gentleman approached Kenneth, asking if the Comanche healer had time to travel to Vermont to meet some of the man's clients. He oversaw a program for hardened juvenile delinquents, gang members, and dangerous young men from the streets of Boston, New York City, and Philadelphia. Kenneth and Rita did not hesitate. They agreed to make the trip into the mountains of Vermont to meet the young men and conduct ceremony. As usual, Kenneth and Rita did not fly to Boston. They had driven their car from Oklahoma to the great city and from Boston they drove through the beautiful landscape of trees, streams, and lakes of the mountains of Vermont.

When Kenneth and Rita reached the camp that housed the young men of many diverse backgrounds, they received a sincere and warm welcome from the administrator they had met in Boston. Once they got settled, Kenneth and Rita went to work constructing a Sweat Lodge from the materials they had brought from Oklahoma, including willow bows, rocks, and canvas. Once they had prepared a roaring fire and began heating the rocks, the campus administrator introduced some of his clients to Kenneth and Rita. They met under the shade of huge leafing trees on a site overlooking the valley below. Kenneth remembers sitting in front of the boys, telling them his personal story and the fundamentals of the Sweat Lodge Ceremony. "While I was telling them about the Sweat Lodge, a little bird came and landed on my shoulder. The boys were amazed. I pretended that the arrival of the bird on my shoulder was no big deal, but really, it amazed me too, but I just kept talking like this happens all the time." The bird remained on Kenneth's shoulder throughout his introduction to the Sweat Lodge Ceremony, and when he finished, he invited all the boys in attendance to join Rita and him in the sweat. Much to his surprise, all of the boys that had heard his talk wanted to join in the ceremony.

"That was one of the most powerful sweats, ever," Kenneth once announced. "When we went in, we sang the Calling and Healing songs given to me by Gracie Black Elk and then began our prayers. While we were in ceremony, we all saw a tiny little mouse come in and climb right into the red-hot rocks. Everybody could see the mouse and we thought it would burn up but it didn't. It was a spirit mouse and after running around in those rocks, that mouse ran out." Not long after the mouse visited the Sweat Lodge Ceremony, Kenneth reported, "A thick blue mist came into the sweat. It crept under the door of the sweat and filled the floor of the Sweat Lodge with blue light." The mist glowed a blue fluorescent just like the blue mist that had surrounded Kenneth's body at Dwight Mission on Sallisaw Creek during the Great Vision. The boys were astonished, said Coosewoon, "and I was so impressed that He came in so strong." Coosewoon received a message to touch the blue light, so he reached down and scooped some of the light substance into his right hand and rubbed the blue essence onto his chest. "I told each of the boys to reach down and take some and put it on their bodies, and they did." The blue light stuck to their chests and Kenneth continued the ceremony, completing the sweat by pouring the remaining water on the rocks and offering a prayer asking the Grandfather to help each and every boy in attendance.

When the ceremony ended, Kenneth and Rita prepared to return home to Oklahoma. During his prayers, Kenneth asked the Grandfather why He had come in so strong for the boys. Coosewoon explained that he received a message: "Those boys had never experienced me in this way and I wanted to come into the Sweat Lodge in a powerful way so they would never forget the ceremony and my presence." To this day, Kenneth would say that the visitation within the Sweat Lodge in the Vermont Mountains was one of the strongest he had ever experienced in his many years of conducting ceremony. Kenneth believes that his many experiences in the Sweat Lodge have prepared him to deal with many different people and forms of illness. The Grandfather, "He prepared me to do this work and help others whether it was those boys or the people that have asked me to pray for them." Kenneth has learned through the words of the Grandfather and through his own experiences, and he uses his innate ability to do the work of healing both inside and outside the holy space of the Sweat Lodge.

Medicine Men

In order to fight illnesses, diseases, and depression brought on by negative energy, the Grandfather had initially armed Coosewoon with his Great Vision and Blue Medicine. Over time, Coosewoon added other items to fight physical, mental, and spiritual infections. Kenneth often uses the Calling and Healing songs and prayers given to him by Wallace and Gracie Black Elk, and he often uses eagle feathers in his healing prayers. Near his home at Medicine Park, Kenneth gathers red berry cedar, sage, and other forms of cedar. He has learned to use sweetgrass, tobacco, and other plant material as part of his medicine when fighting bad medicine and illnesses. During one gathering, a Cheyenne Arrow Keeper gave Kenneth a Talking Stick or Prayer Stick.

At first, Coosewoon did not know how to use the Prayer Stick, but over time he came to understand. He has used the Talking Stick in group sessions, including Sweat Lodge Ceremonies, where he has had people hold it and open their hearts to the Grandfather. During group discussions, Kenneth hands the Talking Stick to a participant and asks the person to use it to say what is on their mind or to pray. He has used the Talking Stick to help those people troubled by negative thoughts, energies, and many forms of illnesses. Over the course of many years, people have given Kenneth many items he has used in ceremony to help others, fulfilling the words of the Grandfather that "all things will come to you, and I will always be with you."

Kenneth has gained a good deal of knowledge about other medicine power by interacting with medicine men and women. Although Kenneth does not recognize himself as a medicine man, most other people see him in this light due to the fact he has power to heal others. At one point in his life, Kenneth Coosewoon was part of a program featuring medicine men, including Arvol Looking Horse, Paul Ortega, Crosslin Smith, and others. Although Kenneth did not borrow from these men or others specific medicine ways, he learned more about Native medicine by listening to their stories and relating their work to help others with his own. Looking Horse, the Keeper of the White Buffalo Calf Pipe, focuses his healings through the sacred pipe of his Lakota people, a shared tradition of many Native Americans of the Great Plains. Crosslin Smith is Cherokee, and he has been a healer for many years, drawing on the traditions of his people to call the power and ask for healing. Paul Ortega is Mescalero Apache. His mother gave him birth during an all-night ceremony held away from the agency. The medicine people leading the ceremony interpreted a massive meteor shower as evidence that the baby would be a man of power. This prophecy came to pass, as Paul Ortega has long possessed the power to heal and help others with their illnesses.

Kenneth's personal experiences confirm his abilities as a healer and medicine man. He has assisted thousands of people, and he continues to answer calls for help. In 2014, a Native American professor from a midwestern university asked Kenneth to help his family. The professor's young son in his first year of life became dangerously ill with pneumonia. When matters looked the most bleak, the professor contacted Coosewoon to ask for healing prayers. According to Kenneth, he began to pray for the child. From his bedroom in Medicine Park, Coosewoon prayed long and often for the child's life. During the winter months when the sun did not shine, Kenneth prayed that the child would be spared. At one point during a prayer, Coosewoon had a calling to walk to his window, a premonition that he followed. After arriving at the window, Kenneth explained, "all of a sudden a strong ray of sunlight broke through and the message came that the boy would live." Coosewoon let the professor, his wife, and family know. Within a few days, the doctors took the boy off the critical list and the little fellow began to recover. The boy lived. He fights asthma but he has gained strength and stamina, as he has gotten older.

Kenneth has worked with many children, especially at the San Marcos Treatment Center in Texas, where he spends weeks on end running a Sweat Lodge and leading prayer ceremonies. Coosewoon has also worked with the House of Life for Children, taking children and adults into the Sweat Lodge. On one occasion, Kenneth and Rita met a woman who wanted to enter the Sweat Lodge but could not bend over and enter the small lodge. "She could not even walk," Kenneth explained, "and she could not bend down and crawl into the Sweat Lodge." So Coosewoon encouraged her to place her wheel chair close to the lodge where she could listen to the songs, hear the prayers, and participate in this removed manner. Before the ceremony, Kenneth prepared prayer ties for her, which he took into the Sweat Lodge and placed in the cross ties of the willows. While in the Sweat Lodge, he prayed for her healing, which came to her. "She got totally healed," Kenneth stated, and the Healing Spirit "totally cured her back problems." According to the Coosewoon, this woman walked away from the Sweat Lodge and left there with no pain.

Successful Healings

Like nearly all of the people Kenneth has helped, he did not know if the woman attending the Sweat Lodge Ceremony at the House of Life had remained pain free. He only would learn of the long-term effects of a healing ceremony if the person communicated with him. He never again heard from this woman. However, Coosewoon enjoys hearing from people he has prayed for and looks forward to letters and telephone calls from people he has helped, including Beverly Patchell.

Years ago, Coosewoon helped Patchell at a Sweat Lodge Ceremony at Oklahoma State University. At this ceremony, Kenneth healed a patient with stage four cancer. During this ceremony, the man prayed for help in preparing to pass, asking the Grandfather to help him prepare for death and to help his family. This man, Kenneth recalled, did not pray for healing, simply assistance. The Healing Spirit intervened in this man's life, healing him of cancer and giving more years to live. For several years, Coosewoon heard from this man. At first the man reported that the cancer had gone into remission and then Kenneth learned the man lived a long, normal life, totally cancer free. The cancer patient had humbled himself before the Grandfather and had received far more than he had asked for in the Sweat Lodge. He received a longer, cancer-free life. Kenneth considers such events truly miraculous brought on by the Healing Spirit and power that exists in the world today. "This is the way the Grandfather works!"

At this same Sweat Lodge Ceremony, Kenneth set Beverly on a healing journey. Kenneth and Beverly became life-long friends, and Coosewoon doctored Beverly through some difficult times over several years. With time, Patchell became an important assistant to Coosewoon, helping him in and out of ceremony. Currently, Patchell is a professor at the University of Utah. Until recently, Beverly had directed the American Indian nursing program at the University of Oklahoma and its College of Nursing. During her tenure with the University of Oklahoma, Beverly brought nursing students and faculty to Medicine Park, Oklahoma, to meet Coosewoon. When appropriate, Kenneth ran a Sweat Lodge Ceremony for students and faculty at the University of Oklahoma to acquaint them with the ancient healing tradition. At one such ceremony, Kenneth took a sheet of paper into the lodge to pray for the names of people listed on the paper. Through the heat and steam, he had a hard time reading the list of people, so he asked generally for healing for all the people listed on the white paper. According to the nurses, all of a sudden Kenneth and the paper he was holding turned a fluorescent blue, the radiant blue Kenneth had seen so often. According to the nurses, Kenneth left the Sweat Lodge but in his absence, the blue glow radiated from the site where he had been seated.

According to Kenneth, his sixth sense has become far more acute with time. The older Coosewoon has gotten, the more he has received detailed messages from the Grandfather. He argues that the messages come to him through psychic words and mental images, although he also reports he also hears the voice of the Grandfather. When working on a patient or dealing with everyday problems of others, Coosewoon "sometimes, but not always," receives a visual picture in his mind of what the patient has experienced. Coosewoon also can feel the pain known by patients, which helps him assist patients. This is especially true of extreme trauma that has harmed the person physically, mentally, or spiritually. Other times, Coosewoon hears things from the spirit world about the patient, especially in the Sweat Lodge.

Kenneth believes the Creator speaks to him specifically, telling him what to do to help the others. "Grandfather speaks directly to me, instructs me." Coosewoon explains, "It's not me." He explains, "It is what non-Indians call God who is "working through me" to help others. "But it's the same thing [God], the tribe's word for Creator." Over the years, Kenneth's ability to see things associated with patients or to hear the words and receive spiritual advice from the Creator has grown and become more pronounced in his everyday life and work.

Abuse of Holy Space

Coosewoon believes that a person must approach the building of every Sweat Lodge in a spiritual manner, and Kenneth has stated emphatically, "no one should ever pay for participating in a ceremony." For Kenneth, selling the right to enter the Sweat Lodge is "sacrilegious" and a violation of the Grandfather. "No one should charge others to come into the Sweat Lodge, because the Grandfather made the lodge for all people," he said. For him, paying for a Sweat Lodge Ceremony is like charging admission to attend a church, synagogue, or mosque. Coosewoon decried the abuse of the Sweat Lodge by Indians and non-Indians alike—people who advertised their use of the Sweat Lodge and charge people to enter the holy space. These same people, sometimes referred to as "Plastic Shaman," often host internet sites, sell hats, t-shirts, and sage where they advertise their new age sweats, charging people and making a mockery of a holy ceremony and space.

This unholy practice is abhorrent to Kenneth, Rita, and every traditionally minded Native American person with knowledge of the ceremony. He especially condemned those that construct the Sweat Lodge incorrectly and with dangerous materials, endangering the lives of participants. For this purpose, he argued that people should construct the Sweat Lodge carefully and approach it in a holy manner. Beverly Patchell once explained, "the form of the Sweat Lodge is not as important as the intent." Although Coosewoon builds his Sweat Lodges in the tradition of Comanche, Lakota, and other Plains people, Patchell felt that diverse forms of the Sweat Lodge exist throughout Indian Country, and Indians from many nations use them in a pragmatic manner to form a sacred space in which to invite the Creator to address the prayers and supplications of participants. It is a sacred place of prayer and healing.

Walking the Good Red Road

On January 9, 2015, Kenneth Coosewoon celebrated his other birthday, the day forty-one years ago when he began to follow the Good Red Road. On that day in 1974, Kenneth stopped drinking and drugging, and he promised himself, his family, and the Grandfather he would never take another drink. The Spirit that had visited in the hospital had told Kenneth, "If you stop drinking, you will live to wear out many blue jeans." The meaning of the message has come to pass. On September 29, 2014, Kenneth celebrated his birthday. At the age of 86, Kenneth's life has unfolded into a series of adventures that included his own family and the great circle of friends and associates he has known for years. He has held healing ceremonies for thousands of men, women, and children. His experiences are many and varied, far too many to share in this record. But Kenneth has left an indelible legacy of a life lived for others. He has shared his prayer with many people of all walks of life and he continues his work to help others.

Over the course of many years now, Kenneth has embraced the Spirit. He has shared the positive aspects of his life with everyone he meets, using his healing gifts to help and benefit others. He has given of himself willingly and freely. In return, Coosewoon has received the gratitude of thousands of people he has healed and counseled for years. During this time, Coosewoon has worked to shed his ego, turning his back on trying to be popular, recognized, or rewarded for his abilities. He has followed a humble approach to life and to his own accomplishment, giving the credit for all healing to the Grandfather. Coosewoon is the first to say that he is human and influenced by people and events around him, but he strives to think of others first and not worry about how others perceive him as a man, father, and healer. He is proud of his Comanche and Kiowa heritage, and he uses his place on earth, as a Native American, to reach the hearts and minds of others. Coosewoon often explains to groups that the Spirit gave him a second chance and a charge. The Spirit directed Kenneth to help, guide, counsel, and heal others. He has spent his life answering this call, but only when asked by people.

Coosewoon never meddles in the lives of others unless people invite him to help them. Unlike some missionaries and evangelists, Coosewoon never pushes his beliefs or ceremonies on people but shares his medicine ways with those interested in learning or healing in his Indian way. Kenneth received power as a result of his encounter with the spirit world, which has guided his life ever since. In fact, Coosewoon believes "different tribes have different beliefs." Kenneth has his own beliefs, based in part on experience and in part on the teachings of the Grandfather. According to Kenneth, the Grandfather taught him about the power and wisdom of the four cardinal directions. Coosewoon explained, "The South is where everything grows, the site of warmth." Grandfather told Kenneth that human beings, plants, and animals "came from Mother Earth, and as we grow, we turn to the West."

Kenneth believes that not everyone moves through the stages of life at the same pace, as "a lot of us take a long time to get to the West" but "when you get to the West, you come into your senses, you start looking within yourself, becoming introspective." Coosewoon said, "that's the Spirit of the West," where people can find the power of "the Eagle, Thunder, and Buffalo." Kenneth's journey to the West took him more time than many people. He explained, "as a boy and as I grew up and finished school, and as I ventured, it took me about thirty years to get to the West because I drank and done everything wrong, jail and everything else and fights. I used to fight all the time. And as I got to the West, I got tired of the way I was living and I started looking within myself and that's when the Great Spirit showed me" the Sweat Lodge Ceremony.

With time and deep thought, Coosewoon came to understand his many problems and "from there, I asked Grandfather to go to the North and face the mighty North Wind." Kenneth asked Grandfather for strength and wisdom, and he began to grow spiritually. "The North is white or red, like the sacred fire of the Sweat Lodge Ceremony. It is also where the white snow lives. When you get to the North, you are growing as a person and you learn more. From the North, a person turns toward the East to learn wisdom and knowledge. It's when you are older, you've been through most of it." From there, a person turns back to the Mother Earth where we originated in spiritual form. In this way, humans "complete the whole circle." At that point, you are whole, a full circle. Kenneth Coosewoon believes he has made a journey in his life, traveling the four directions and learning all the while. He has not completed the circle and continues to learn, just as he had when he was younger, learning and growing in the Spirit.

Singing for Dr. Van Brocklyn

A few years ago, the wife of Dr. Van Brocklyn, a former professor at the University of Oklahoma, contacted the Cherokee Nation headquarters to ask for a medicine man to help her. People in the main office of Chief Wilma Mankiller called Kenneth to ask as favor. Mrs. Van Brocklyn explained that her husband had died and had been cremated. She told Kenneth that her father had always had a deep and sincere belief in the spiritual ways of the Native Americans, and she wanted his remains to be spread on Tecumseh Mountain in a Native American ceremony. Kenneth told her, "No, I had never done nothing like that." Then Kenneth asked for her husband's name, and when she said, Van Brocklyn, Kenneth recognized the name. He had worked with Dr. Van Brocklyn, a psychologist, when Coosewoon led the drug and alcohol treatment center at the old Fort Sill Indian School. After learning the identity of the deceased, Kenneth agreed to do ceremony for Dr. Van Brocklyn, although he was unsure how to do the ceremony.

"I prayed to the Grandfather and asked if this was ok," Kenneth remembered. "I told Grandfather, I need to know what to do." The answer came clear to Kenneth, saying he should help the family and pray over the remains of the good doctor in his own way. The Grandfather gave Kenneth basic help but Kenneth remembered that He had told him during the Great Vision, "I will always be with you and will always help you." Kenneth trusted in these reminders and he drove to Tecumseh Mountain with an open mind and heart. Coosewoon and Rita worked together to do ceremony for Dr. Van Brocklyn while Mrs. Van Brocklyn, her daughter, and Mr. Richard Downey looked on. When they reached the top of the mountain, Kenneth began the ceremony by lighting a roll of sage he had brought from the Southern Plains. Coosewoon hung the sage roll in a tree before he and Rita began to sing the Calling and Healing songs. They prayed for the deceased and the living, asking for help and healing. Coosewoon then lit some red berry cedar, setting it down near the remains of Dr. Van Brocklyn. All the while, Kenneth used his eagle feather and prayed for the psychologist. All of a sudden, the cedar gave out a loud hissing noise and every eye turned toward the cedar, which ascended into the air and danced back and forth, all the while smoking its sweet aroma. Then Kenneth said a prayer out loud. "Grandfather, if it is possible, please turn Dr. Van Brocklyn into an eagle so he may fly above these beautiful mountains and see the earth." As Kenneth concluded his prayer, an eagle appeared in the sky overhead, screeching its voice to let the world know Kenneth's prayer had been heard.

In recent times, Coosewoon has used his spiritual medicine to help a young woman sick from a broken relationship. One evening under the stars and beside a small campfire, Kenneth prayed for this young woman to stop drinking and to pull her life back together. Coosewoon told her parents that she would be fine within a short time and begin a new path. Within a few months after the prayers and smudging, the young woman stopped drinking, returned to university, and began a new job as manager of a clothing store.

Kenneth also prayed for two good men who were dying of cancer. Although his prayers did not result in the curing of cancer, Kenneth's actions touched both men deeply and they received a form of divine healing that helped them during their last days. Kenneth also responded to another request to send a medicine bundle to a young woman taken suddenly ill with cancer in her vital organs. She lived through a lengthy, complicated surgery and has responded positively to radiation treatment. Her case is pending, but Coosewoon did not hesitate to ask for healing and to pray daily for this young woman.

These are but a few examples of the way Kenneth Coosewoon continues his work as a holy man and healer. His life centers around the Grandfather and prayer. Coosewoon is limited in his own movement due to injured knees and hips, but he sets aside time each day to pray for people in need and to answer the call of people from every walk of life, asking for his help to heal the people they love. According to their family, Kenneth and Rita Coosewoon "continue to share their passion for helping people and they remain a powerful spiritual duo, often attending events and running sweats in tandem."

Chapter 2
Time of Spirit and Healing
By Ronald Cooper

For me, Kenneth's path to Native American spirituality couldn't have come at a better time. I was about seventeen and I had just read the classic *Bury My Heart at Wounded Knee,* the iconic book about the destruction of the Native American way of life. I figured I could have gone down one of two paths after reading this book: I could either fill my heart with hatred for what the white man did to us, or I could demonstrate to the world that we Indians weren't entirely gone from the face of the earth. I chose the latter.

This photograph depicts a family scene with Kenneth sitting in the chair. Surrounding Kenneth from left to right is his daughter, Raylyn, Doraline, Jaime, and daughter, Deanna.

I began studying the culture my ancestors had fought so hard to preserve. Gone, especially from my Comanche culture, were the ceremonies and rituals specific to my tribe. However, I believed that if I could understand what my ancestors had thought about the world around them that I could connect with them in that manner. I learned as much as I could about the Native American system of values and thought processes regarding the Great Spirit, Mother Earth, and other spiritual beliefs. Once I began that process it became clear that I wanted some kind of ceremony to connect my present with the past of my ancestors.

That ceremony came in the form of the Sweat Lodge. Without my knowing it at the time, Kenneth was learning about the Sweat Lodge independently from my self-education. The Sweat Lodge (sometimes shortened to "the sweat" or "sweats") is a universal ceremony in all Native American cultures. Some say it is the oldest ritual in our history, along with fasting, to connect with the Great Spirit. Many times the Sweat Lodge is used as a purification ceremony to begin other events deemed important in a given Native society. Other times, it can be a rite unto itself. Because our old Comanche ceremonies are lost to us, we choose to use the Sweat Lodge as a stand-alone event.

I have seen many mysterious things in the Sweat Lodge but my first experience occurred without me even being in one. Kenneth had gone to see Lakota medicine man Wallace Black Elk at a gathering at Oklahoma's Dwight Mission. There, Kenneth would get to know this man and learn many things about Native American spirituality. Black Elk gave my grandfather some Lakota songs to sing in the Sweat Lodge, used to call upon the spirits to come into our ceremony and help us by answering prayers and to heal any sicknesses we or our loved ones may have at the time. This was crucial to me because I had been battling a stomach ailment that the doctors could not diagnose until it was too late.

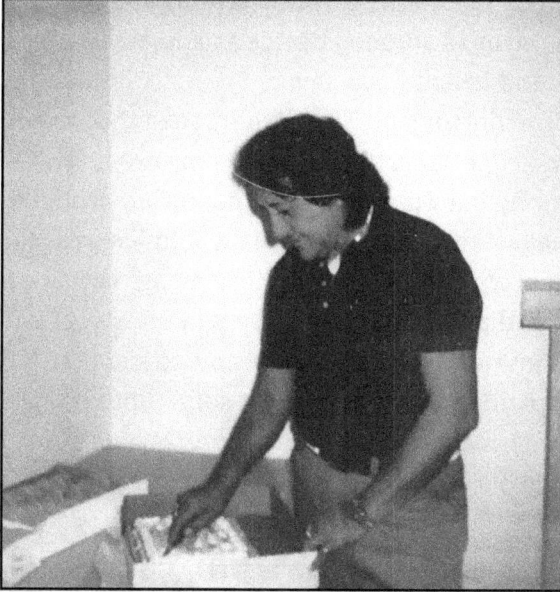

Each year on January 9th, Kenneth, his family, and his friends celebrate his second birthday. On January 9, 1974, Kenneth stopped drinking, and so every January the Coosewoon family celebrates this important date when he started walking the Good Red Road.

While I was being rushed into the emergency room for what was most likely a ruptured appendix (I didn't display the classic symptoms), Kenneth was in the Sweat Lodge with Black Elk. During prayers and song, Black Elk told Kenneth that I would be okay even though it would be a struggle. What makes this statement so extraordinary is that Kenneth never told him about me. My appendix surgery did not go as planned. A normal 30-minute procedure took three hours because doctors could not find my appendix! Instead of rupturing, my appendix had rotted and shriveled to a point where it had simply fallen off and was lost within the rest of my organs. Surgeons had to make two other cuts to my abdomen to look for it. A specialist was about to be called in when the head surgeon decided to do another search. He finally found it, and I was saved.

The doctor said, "I have only seen this one other time—in deepest, darkest Africa!" I'm sure he was exaggerating but the rarity of my condition brought home the fact that if my appendix would have ruptured the normal way, I might not be here today. I attribute my survival to the power of the prayers in the Sweat Lodge. With my grandfather I have been able to see first-hand the unexplained occurrences that sometimes happen in Native American rituals. He mentions a "blue glow" when describing his vision and I was able to see it myself on several occasions.

This photograph was taken outside one sunny day. Kenneth is sporting a white suit. Accompanying Kenneth to the right in the photograph is daughter, Deanna, Kenneth's mother, Mattie, and Doraline.

When my Uncle Jaime was shot and almost died of his injuries, Kenneth and I went into the Sweat Lodge one night to pray for his recovery. An owl, a messenger to many Native American cultures, told me that although he is close to death, he would be okay. I can only describe this message as a thought, not an actual voice. Kenneth said the owl had also talked to him and told him the same thing.

As we came out of the lodge Kenneth looked down the embankment at the creek below us. He saw the blue glow and showed it to me. It wasn't too difficult to see for long because the glow began to light up along both banks of the creek. All this was a good sign for us and my uncle who gained strength.

After some touch and go moments my uncle recovered from his injuries. In one Sweat Lodge Ceremony, I sat beside Kenneth during the session. Before the last one he noticed the blue glow on the ground between us. He took some and put it on my leg. I touched some to see how it felt but it had no substance at all. I rubbed it on my chest and we closed the door to begin the last session. The other participants described seeing my entire body as it glowed blue in the darkness. Neither I nor Kenneth know what the blue glow is or its true significance, except we knew it was spiritual in nature. We do know that it is somehow connected to the Great Spirit and that's good enough for us.

The blue glow isn't the only supernatural thing that has occurred in my grandfather's Sweat Lodges. We have seen what appeared to be the "universe" inside the sweat. One evening we had a sweat under a full moon. Our friend David acted as our "rock boy"—what we call the person who gets the rocks out of the fire to transfer them into the pit inside the lodge. He commented on how full the moon looked

At an American Indian conference, a photographer took a picture of Rita and Kenneth Coosewoon, in the center of the image. The two unidentified women on either side of Kenneth and Rita were attendees of the conference who wanted to take their photograph with the Coosewoons.

on this night as it shone brightly above us. Kenneth said off-handedly, "Then bring it in here with us." David said okay and we laughed, closed the door, and began our last session for the night.

We were in the Sweat Lodge no more than 20 minutes and when we came out, the moon was gone! We couldn't believe our eyes! Our first thought was that the moon had set past our horizon but surely it could not have gone from directly above and disappear in 20 minutes. We finally concluded the "impossible." The moon decided to take us up on our offer and joined us for the last session of our sweat. The stars once came into our Sweat Lodge as well. Our group was sitting in the Sweat Lodge after the sessions were over. It was dark out except for the light of the fire glowing through the open door. We looked up and it seemed as if someone had taken the top off the lodge revealing the starry night sky. I'm sure it was the way the light danced within the lodge but it was very realistic to all of us, and certainly did not look like a trick of the eye.

Other happenings I have experienced with Kenneth in the Sweat Lodge can run into the category of the mundane, yet still be significant. At that time I was working with my grandfather, who would travel around the country to build and perform sweats for different organizations, groups, or just individuals who needed it. In doing so, many times we would improvise on the material to cover the Sweat Lodge frame. This time we used plastic trash bags to cover the willow frame, then we would put our main cover over that. Since we had gotten there late we decided to build the lodge that evening and then hold the ceremony the next night. Overnight, a moderate rain had fallen — just enough to cool the following summer day but not enough to cancel our sweat.

This was a great night to hold a sweat and the first three sessions went off without a hitch. On the last session we re-entered the lodge, closed the door and began. As Kenneth was finishing up his words, he turned to where his water bucket usually is, in order to sprinkle water on the hot rocks which creates the steam. We had forgotten to bring it back in with us. Fortunately, the spirits helped us out.

The overnight rains had leaked under the main canvas cover where some had collected in the plastic trash bag material we put underneath. Right above the rock pit we had noticed a little reservoir of water hanging there, but at the time we thought nothing of it. Just as Kenneth noted we had forgotten to bring in the water bucket, a small flame shot up from the rocks and touched the plastic. That opened a hole for the water to come pouring onto the rocks. It created a nice steam and no scalding water hit anybody in the sweat. The water was just enough for us to continue our last session without having to get the bucket for more water. The flame confounded me the most, because there is nothing in the pit that could have caused a flash of fire like that.

The flame touching the plastic and causing the rainwater to drop was not a miracle by any stretch of the imagination, but it does make you think about what goes on in the Sweat Lodge. What I think is most important about Kenneth's Sweat Lodge is that everyone is invited. Black Elk once told us, "When a spirit comes into the Sweat Lodge, it doesn't say, 'I am a white person's spirit,' or 'I am an Indian spirit.' The Sweat Lodge is for everyone, no matter what color they are or where they are from."

There are no specific rituals to follow in Kenneth's Sweat Lodge, no taboos to fear. We simply go in to feel the toxins leave our bodies as the sweat drips from our pores. We hear other people's prayers and say our own, without any fear of judgment. When we're in the Sweat Lodge the rest of the world gets blocked off and only the group participating in the ceremony and the Great Spirit remains. Participants are truly isolated from the temporal and contemporary world. It's that way out of necessity but it works for the clientele that Kenneth brings into the sweat. The necessity is that our sweat is a collection of pieces of other tribes' ceremonies. The first impression may seem odd for a Comanche holy man to be singing Lakota songs in the sweat, but that's the way my grandfather learned and it works. There are no specific steps to follow because he doesn't know any. There is always a "multi-denominational" theme to his sweat. Many different tribal members have participated in his sweats and each tribe has different Sweat Lodge etiquette. It works better in Kenneth's sweat that there is no dogma, just an open, direct, and honest connection between participants and the Grandfather. One learns the basics of the Sweat Lodge with Kenneth, and if a more specific tribal ritual is desired then that person can go to a tribe and learn their ways. The sincerity of the prayers in the sweat is the goal in Kenneth's Sweat Lodge, not the way the prayers are said.

My grandfather's main gift to those who visit him and participate in his Sweat Lodge is the power of the unconditional love he has for people. He believes that everyone should receive the benefit of the doubt. According to Kenneth, anyone can be forgiven from transgressions and be transformed into a new person. Everybody is good deep down and everyone can get help from the prayers in the Sweat Lodge—if they believe strongly enough.

This is a family photograph of Kenneth's two daughters with their maternal grandmother, Aline Taylor. In this image, Raylyn appears on the left side of Doraline's mother, while Deanna is shown to the right of her grandmother.

Chapter 3
Learning the Medicine Way
with Kenneth Coosewoon
By Beverly Patchell

Kenneth grew up on Kiowa land that had been allotted to his mother, Mattie Kauley Coosewoon, and currently lives in a house next door to that land. Throughout his life he roamed the land, learning to ride a horse at age three, and to hunt for food for his family. He learned to shoot a gun at an early age and killed his first deer at age five. He killed his first deer with a .22 caliber single shot rifle. That day he and his mother were out and got stranded in Medicine Park during a snowstorm. They went to Kenneth's aunt's house nearby to wait out the storm, but needed food. His mother sent Kenneth out into the storm to shoot a rabbit for them, but instead he shot a deer. It was frequently his job to go out and hunt small game so they could have meat for their meals. Comanche and Kiowa are meat eaters, and Kenneth helped the family hunt a fair share of the game the family ate. Kenneth was a crack shot, so he became the principle supplier of wild game. His younger cousins would go out with him to carry the game back.

Kenneth's father, Abner Coosewoon, was a farmer and was busy plowing, seeding, weeding, and harvesting, leaving the hunting to Kenneth. His parents met at boarding school and eventually got married. They had three daughters during their marriage and Kenneth was a change-of-life baby and a surprise to his parents. There was a 10-year age difference between him and the next oldest sibling. All of his sisters went to boarding school, but he did not. His mother opted to keep him at home and sent him to the local one room schoolhouse from first thru eighth grades. Kenneth went to public schools and graduated from Elgin High School located near Lawton, Oklahoma in the heart of Comanche and Kiowa Country. Early family life memories include being very poor. He was born during the Great Depression when his family had to find their own food. Fortunately for Kenneth and his family, he was a superior hunter, providing meat for his immediate and extended family. His mother also had to sell some of her inherited land to help provide for them, and she beaded beautiful art work to help the family, selling her beadwork to interested parties. Mattie's mother, Kenneth's grandmother, lost her father early on and her mother remarried a white man. He took control of all of their land and money, sent her children off to boarding schools or to relatives and then they started another family. By the time his mother was married, she had very little left of what was intended to be hers.

As a young boy, while roaming around the land, Kenneth slid down a cliff, which could have killed him. But his friends had a rope that they tossed down to Kenneth which he used to climb up out of the gorge that had entrapped him. They often killed rattlesnakes while out because they were everywhere. He remembered that there is a sacred place back in the mountains that he found as a boy. It was notable because "the stream ran backward," the only one in the area that went from south to north. He has always longed to go back and find that place because now he believes it is a place of strong medicine.

His first driver's license was a commercial license, and in 1946 Kenneth got a job driving a school bus. His new job paid him $30 each month, which was a lot of money at that time. The money helped his family and provided Kenneth the only cash he had access to for gas and other things. His mother had some money, but she gave most of it to the Methodist Church in their community. Although she was generous to the church, they did not help her or even come to see her when she was ill, turning Kenneth against the Christian religion for a long time.

Beverly Patchell proudly stands in front of the sign indicating the Cherokee Nation. She is holding an abalone shell, which she uses when burning sage, cedar, or sweetgrass. In the photograph to her right is one of the students from the Sequoyah campus. He is holding a drum used to accompany songs.

As a freshman in high school, Kenneth played varsity sports in track, basketball, and baseball. Although Kenneth was a natural athlete and one that loved sports, he found himself searching for an identity and true spirit. He began drinking alcohol at age 14 to 15 and he described how he could hear his mother praying for him to quit drinking every night before she would go to bed. Kenneth's mother desperately wanted him to go to church, which he would not do. When he began training for boxing in 1948-1949, he stopped drinking. After high school he went to Cameron College (now Cameron University), but was drafted at age 21 and also married before going into the United States Army. About six months into the service, he hurt his shoulder badly while throwing grenades and was honorably discharged.

Back at home, he worked in construction and became a truck driver to make a living. In 1952 he went to dry cleaning school and was hired by Griswald's Dry Cleaning in Lawton, Oklahoma. He worked at Griswald's until 1958. He then went to work for the Fort Sill dry cleaner's, but was fired for drinking too much and being undependable. As a result of his firing, Kenneth sobered up and went back to work there for two years. Then Kenneth and Doraline opened their own dry cleaning business, calling it Ken's Cleaners. He was successful, but began to drink again after a couple of years and drank for 10 more years. He also fought with people over anything and everything, sometimes fighting someone just to fight. He also had multiple car accidents and cannot account for his ability to walk away from so many deadly accidents. Doraline eventually could not tolerate Kenneth's behavior anymore and kicked him out. She packed some clothes in a large Kotex box and set it out on the porch. This was her signal to Kenneth to go and not come back.

Over the course of many years, Kenneth, Doraline, Rita, Ron Cooper, and Beverly Patchell traveled thousands of miles to take the Sweat Lodge Ceremony to hundreds of people. When they traveled to do ceremony, they cut their own willows, which they took with them on top of their cars to use for the frame of the Sweat Lodge. In addition, they also took their own rocks that they had gathered from their homeland. Both willows and rocks are integral parts of the ceremony and considered sacred elements to many Native Americans.

Kenneth left home, but soon became dangerously depressed. He recalls becoming suicidal. He ran his car into a tree in an attempt to kill himself. He fought with anyone and everyone, not caring if they killed him or not. He even fought with the police. He became so distraught that he decided to commit suicide by carbon monoxide poisoning. On his way walking toward a site where he could end his life, his brother-in-law pulled up alongside of Kenneth and told him Doraline wanted him to come home. She did not know it at the time, but her timing saved Kenneth's life. So Kenneth returned home with his wife and two girls, but he continued to drink. At that time he had been drinking steadily and heavily for ten years, which caused him to become weaker and sicker. He drank so much he passed out easily, and even Kenneth worried he was getting "red brained."

One day Kenneth passed out at home and woke up in the hospital. Attendants at the hospital had tied him down so he would not hurt anyone or himself. At that time Kenneth was having delirium tremens. He saw Little People running around his room, laughing at him. Grandfather came to him and told him to quit drinking now and he would live to wear out many blue jeans, but if he did not, he would die. With a sobriety date of January 9, 1974, Kenneth returned to Alcoholics Anonymous (AA) with an Osage man his brother-in-law had introduced him to. Kenneth remembers that at first he was afraid to go to AA, with all of those white people, because he did not know how they would treat him. He felt "like a little boy," but was able to go with the help of the Osage man. When he arrived at the AA meeting, he saw many other Indians and realized they had similar stories to his own. When his mother asked him how AA helped when the church did not, he told her it was because he felt accepted there and not judged.

When Kenneth constructs a Sweat Lodge, he places the door of the lodge to the East, facing the rising sun. This photograph depicts Kenneth beginning construction of a Sweat Lodge with two willow branches that he will attach to two corresponding willow approximately ten feet from these two willows.

I originally met Kenneth and Rita Coosewoon when they came to a ROPES Conference in 1989 near Stillwater, Oklahoma, to conduct Sweat Lodge ceremonies. I was unable to attend the Sweat during the conference because I was on my moon at the time. Not long afterwards, they invited me to come to the Sweats they did at a treatment center for adolescents at Arcadia, Oklahoma. I attended many Sweats there with them as they came regularly to do them for the patients and staff. Several people who had life threatening illnesses came to Kenneth's Sweat Lodge Ceremonies, and they were healed. I witnessed many miracles. The patients were always respectful and helpful. Kenneth and Rita affected the lives of many people by the work they did there. A friend David often accompanied Kenneth and Rita to the Sweats. He helped with the fire, providing the Sweats with hot rocks. They worked as a team and conducted Sweat Lodge Ceremonies all over Oklahoma. I attended many that Kenneth and Rita held near to me; sites to which I could easily drive.

At almost every sweat that Kenneth conducted, someone was healed of something, from back pain to cancer. Over time, I came to know Kenneth's and Rita's families as well as their community. I also began to learn how powerful the Sweat Lodge was if utilized as a healing force for Grandfather/Creator. My knowledge of the Sweat Lodge of Kenneth and Rita helped me in my personal and professional life. In fact, my knowledge of the Sweat Lodge would soon influence my personal work for the Cherokee Nation. In 1990, I went to work for the Jack Brown Treatment Center in Tahlequah, Oklahoma, as a part-time family therapist. When I was first hired, I worked two to three days each week. Within a year, I was willing to take the position full-time and was in the process of moving to Tahlequah, when the Director resigned and I was asked to take over. I directed the program and enjoyed working for my tribal people, the Cherokee, and living in close proximity to my birthplace in Tahlequah, Oklahoma.

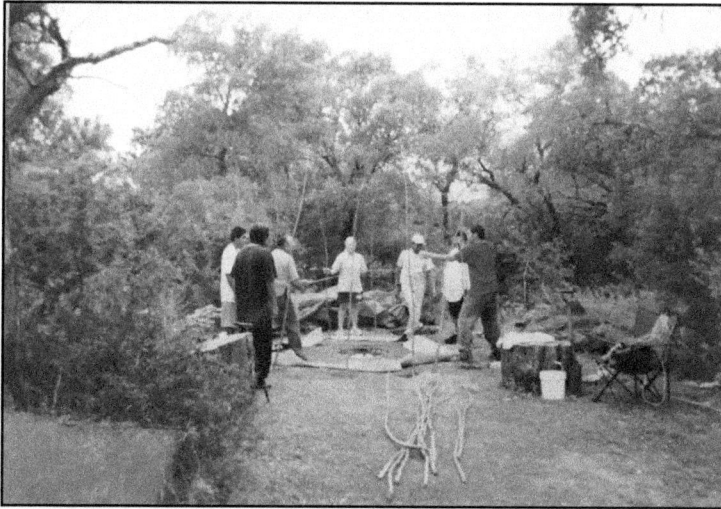

Kenneth feels that participants in his Sweat Lodge Ceremonies will gain a greater appreciation of the ceremony if they help build the lodge. Often, Kenneth remembers the first Sweat Lodge he helped build on Cache Creek at the Fort Sill Indian School when his clients suggested they create the "little church."

The Jack Brown Center is an adolescent treatment center operated by the Cherokee Nation of Oklahoma and funded through the Indian Health Service. The Jack Brown Center remains in Oklahoma today, helping young people find their way in life. When I became Director, the Center had very few patients and one of my foremost early tasks required me to increase the census. Simply put, we needed to serve more people, so I worked diligently to increase the number of young people we served. In making changes to accommodate more patients, I asked Kenneth and Rita to come to work there, starting part-time. I asked them to offer a healing modality that I knew the adolescents would benefit from. The Center was in an old building on the campus of the boarding school operated by the Cherokee Nation and could hold 25 patients. In years past, the building had been an orphanage, a mental institution, and a hospital all operated by the federal government.

Many patients and children, often disturbed by negative aspects of their lives, lived at this boarding school facility at various times in the past. I knew the area well because my grandfather had worked for the boarding school, operating the coal furnaces that provided heat for the school buildings. The old boarding school was haunted and filled with lost spirits. The ghosts and entities of this site often manifested themselves to the children at the school, moving objects, making noises, and appearing through mists and shadows. The presence of the paranormal at the boarding school proved troubling for the staff and students alike. The staff and patients of the Center had to deal with the lost spirits from the past history of the building. I often received reports of staff and young people hearing babies crying, people moaning, and being unable to sleep due to feeling pressure placed on their bodies while our patients were in bed.

In order to deal with these spiritual issues found within the buildings, Kenneth Coosewoon would often go through the building with cedar and sage, smudging the rooms and the building as a whole. He would use his eagle feather and prayers to move from the rooms to hallways and other rooms, using his medicine power to drive out these lost spirits out of the building. He also smudged the patients and staff, praying to Grandfather to drive the negative spirits out of the rooms and away from the children. During our work at the Jack Brown Center, we all would see dark shadows fly out of closets and out of the bedrooms of the patients. The night staff kept a log of things heard and seen on the night shift. They regularly recorded noises and sightings of shadow people. At one point a Cherokee medicine man told us that we could never get rid of all the spirits because the building was on the site of a playground of the Little People, and they would not stay away for long. We just tried to live peaceably with them, but rid ourselves and the building of those spirits causing pain and suffering.

For many years, Ronald Cooper, Kenneth's grandson, has helped build Sweat Lodges and conduct ceremonies to benefit others. Kenneth raised Ronald in the ceremony and they have led many ceremonies over several years. Notice that this Sweat Lodge has many willows lashed together, tying the frame together. In addition, this photograph clearly shows the rock pit in the center of the lodge.

During the early 1990s, the census grew at the Jack Brown Center. Unfortunately, this was a time when the gang movement was in full swing in most communities, especially California. The Center often received Native American adolescents who were from these gangs and whose way of life was violent and filled with drug abuse. These young people did not like following any rules and were difficult to handle. We developed a process of picking them up at the airport about 90 miles away, bringing them straight to the Sweat Lodge for an introduction to spirituality before setting foot in the Center. They did not have to go into the Sweat Lodge, but they did have to sit outside where they could hear the prayers of the staff and other adolescents asking for their acceptance of the healing being offered. If they did go into the Sweat Lodge, they often cried and said they had given their soul to the Devil and were doomed to go to hell.

When Kenneth and Rita heard the young people confess to giving their souls to Satan, the spiritual healers told the patients that they were not doomed to Hell. This revelation, given by two powerful prayer leaders and holy people, proved life changing for these young people. Once the young people had gone into the Sweat Lodge or had participated outside, they were then taken to the Center. We took them into the Jack Brown Center to take care of them, provide them security, and introduce them into the community. Any patient who lost control and had to go and do a timeout in their room, would immediately receive a visit from Kenneth.

When Kenneth went to talk with unruly patients, they immediately calmed down and listened to what Kenneth had to say. He told them about his early life and how wild he had been at their age. Kenneth took his time and calmly explained his own spirituality and how his work with Grandfather to help other people had changed his life. Kenneth would tell the young people that the gifts given to him helped him become a better person and were available to them. He asked them to consider allowing Grandfather to enter their lives. It was a great privilege for the patients to receive the unconditional support and help of Kenneth or Rita Coosewoon who truly care about other human beings and show it every day. Kenneth and Rita conducted Sweat Lodge Ceremonies for the patients, and within a short time after arriving at the Jack Brown Center, they were doing three to four Sweats a week, with scheduled Sweat Lodge Ceremonies for the boys, the girls, and the staff. They might also be called upon to do Sweats for guests of the Principal Chief of the Cherokee Nation or for someone who had experienced an illness or a relative needing assistance. Kenneth and Rita conducted Sweat Lodge Ceremonies rain or shine throughout the year. One memorable ceremony was during the Cherokee National Holiday in the early 1990s.

Chief Wilma Mankiller had asked Kenneth to do a Sweat Lodge for her guests at the holiday. So we did and later learned one of the people there was Gloria Steinem and several famous artists. He didn't really know who she was, but said it didn't matter. Kenneth always said everyone was equal and looked the same inside the Sweat Lodge anyway. In 1998, they finally retired from the Jack Brown Center, but it wasn't long before Kenneth was conducting ceremonies for the children at the San Marcos Treatment Center in San Marcos, Texas. He has been traveling to San Marcos and working with their children ever since, and he continues to spend time conducting Sweat Lodge for the children there, especially during the Christmas week. Kenneth is selfless when sharing his healing gifts with young people and anyone that asks for his assistance.

Kenneth enjoys remembering his life and often shares his stories with groups of people and me. He told about a time as a child when he went to the grocery store with his

In this photograph, Ronald Cooper helps Kenneth lash the ribs of the Sweat Lodge together. Before beginning the ceremony, Kenneth wraps several stands of tobacco ties, which he places in the ribs of the lodge. He prays for people while he wraps each tobacco tie and continues the prayer as he places the ties in the Sweat Lodge.

mother and they bought raw kidneys. The clerk was curious and asked Mattie how she cooked the kidneys. She told him an elaborate story about slicing them, flouring them, then putting them in hot grease to fry. Then they went out to the car and ate the kidneys raw, laughing about how the clerk would not understand about eating raw food. Another story also took place at a butcher shop. While his parents were talking to the butcher and other customers, young Kenneth would walk into the area where the butcher had hung up the split carcasses of animals. Kenneth would quietly pull out the spinal cords and put them in a sack he had brought along and carried the spinal cords to the car. When his parents returned to the car, Kenneth and his folks would eat those raw, too. Kenneth also liked to tell about how he and his friends would work over the butchered lower legs of cows.

After they were butchered, the boys would chew up the end of a willow twig and use it as a probe to sweep the marrow out of the broken leg bones. He also caught large turtles, which they just threw into the oven to cook. Once cooked, Kenneth and his friends and family would break open the turtle shells and eat the meat. He caught frogs and hand-fished for food, too. Kenneth commented that he had learned as a young boy to fish only with his hands, catching fish and bringing them home to eat.

Kenneth's paternal grandfather was Mexican. Comanche raiders had captured Kenneth's Dad's father as a child in Mexico. The Comanche had adopted Kenneth's grandfather into the tribe. He had grown up in the Comanche community, and he only knew the Comanche language. He was raised as a Comanche and he was always accepted as a Comanche man. Kenneth's grandfather had four wives but when the United States Army forced the Comanche tribe onto the reservation, military leaders and superintendents of Indian affairs told him that he could only have one wife. As a result, Kenneth's paternal grandmother had to leave her husband and family, although she took her son—Kenneth's father—with her when she left. Her name was Coosewoon, the name that Kenneth's father, Abner Coosewoon, used. Abner kept his mother's name, which became the family name for Kenneth and his siblings and children.

Kenneth says because of this large extended family on both sides, he was always concerned about being too closely related to Comanche or Kiowa girls. He worried that they might be a relative. To marry them would be a violation of traditional Comanche and Kiowa marriage laws. Kenneth once met an Apache girl while he was away on a work detail in Arizona and almost brought her home as his wife, but ultimately chose not to do so. When he was 21, he married 15-year-old Doraline Taylor. He had just gotten drafted into the Army and they wanted to be married. Neither set of parents was happy about the match. Doraline's folks were unhappy because she was marrying an Indian. Kenneth's parents were unhappy because he was marrying a white girl. Her parents eventually relented and stood up for them. Kenneth and Doraline lived with her parents during his military time and right afterward. By then, Kenneth had a reputation as a fierce fighter and was often asked to go out by his cousins. They knew no one would bother them if he was there. He once got a job as a bouncer because he beat up the bouncer who had tried to throw him out.

Many styles of Sweat Lodge exist. Kenneth uses the style of Sweat Lodge known to Comanche, Kiowa, and most people of the Great Plains. He uses the oiled canvas of former tents to place over the frame of the lodge. In this way, the canvas keeps in the heat and steam generated when water hits the red-hot rocks, which permeates the body bringing an element of the holy into the pores of each participant. This photograph illustrates one style of Sweat Lodge and the style used by Kenneth Coosewoon.

After his mother became elderly and ill, Kenneth and his wife Doraline took care of her in their house next door. Right before her death, one of Kenneth's sisters talked her into signing a new will, giving her and her children all of the mother's assets. When Mattie realized what had been done, his mother asked Kenneth to take her to the office of the Bureau of Indian Affairs to change it back. She explained to Kenneth that she wanted him to have the house. Kenneth told her no, he did not want to fight with his sister about it. After her death, his sister moved in and had parties with lots of drinking and carrying on in the house. The sister eventually became ill and moved out. Kenneth said the house has always been haunted and no one has really been able to live in it. He thinks his mother still wants him to have it and won't let anyone else settle in there.

In 1999, Doraline was struck down one day by a heart attack. Kenneth knew she was ready to pass on, because as she was lying on the floor after the attack, she told him she was going. Doraline told Kenneth to keep doing the Sweat Lodge and not to stop. She tenderly told him that she loved him. He was grief-stricken and depressed for a long time afterward. At one point he had a gun loaded and cocked, ready to kill himself. But Grandfather came to him and said, "don't do it Kenneth, not like this. Doraline is happy, not in any pain, she says to tell you to remember what she said about continuing to do your work." He knew then that Doraline was with Grandfather and that he should keep going. He sold the gun and moved back into life. Kenneth and Rita continued to work closely together doing Sweat Lodge Ceremony. Rita was with him constantly and he felt like they should be married and so they married about the year 2003. Kenneth claimed he was tired of all the other women in the community chasing him as he was a very eligible widower at that time! Besides, Rita had promised Doraline she would take care of Kenneth, so it seemed like the thing to do. They have been happily married ever since.

In March 2005 Kenneth and Rita were scheduled to speak at the Medicine Ways Conference at the University of Oklahoma. Shortly before the conference, Kenneth became ill and was having tremendous pain. He finally asked to be taken to the Indian hospital emergency room in Lawton, Oklahoma. Doctors in the ER thought Kenneth might be having a heart attack, and they sent him by ambulance from Lawton to an Oklahoma City hospital, about 75 miles away. They would not give him any pain medicine since they were not sure what was going on, so he felt every bump and was in great pain the entire trip. In Oklahoma City, they decided it was his gallbladder and sent him back to Lawton. Rita took him home, then back to the hospital, where they gave him an appointment in two weeks. Rita refused to leave until a doctor saw him, so finally one did and decided he needed immediate surgery. He was sent to the community hospital, where it was determined that his gallbladder had ruptured, and he promptly went into surgery.

While in surgery Kenneth said he died and went to heaven where he saw his wife and mother. It was so peaceful that he wanted to stay. Grandfather told him he could stay or go. It was up to him. He decided to return because he felt like he needed to come back for his daughters, to help them get their lives straightened up. He then woke up in the hospital, but he was at peace with it because he knew he would eventually return to be with Grandfather. Rita stayed with him throughout his days in the hospital, making sure he was well cared for. She came to the conference and spoke, telling their story and talking about medicine and healing. It is there that she and I met Cliff Trafzer. Over the years, Cliff has become a partner in this medicine journey and the faithful recorder of these medicine ways. One of his first experiences with Kenneth's healing was for a friend. Shortly after meeting Kenneth, he asked Kenneth to pray for a friend just diagnosed with breast cancer and so Kenneth did that. He also gave Cliff a medicine bag and medicine to give to her. At her next checkup, she was cancer free.

Kenneth stands near the fire set up to heat the rocks used in the Sweat Lodge. Notice that Kenneth uses long, thick logs situated in a circular fashion, tipi like, around the rocks with a great deal of kindling in the middle of the circle near the rocks. The fire generates a great deal of heat that creates high temperatures. At the start of the ceremony, the "rock boy" carries the rocks from the fire outside into the lodge, placing them in the center of the Sweat Lodge.

It was at the Jack Brown Center that I really began to "study" with Kenneth and Rita and began an apprentice journey that carried me into the next century as I learned the ways of the Sweat Lodge and healing with Grandfather. Participating in two to three sweats each week quickly advanced my ability to connect with the healing spirit and use it to help others. I had already learned much from my paternal grandfather, who also was a Native healer, and who taught me how to pray, hunt and forage for healing plants. Kenneth's advice to me to "pray with every step" brought back my memories of those sunrise prayers with my grandfather as he talked to me about getting along in this world. My husband and young sons were also close to Kenneth and Rita and we all went on several journeys together to visit other areas, such as Albuquerque, Las Vegas, and North Carolina.

My sons had their first Sweat Lodge experience with Kenneth and Rita on the banks of the Baron Fork Creek near Tahlequah when they were seven and five years old. We were holding a sweat out on the creek bank because one of the Jack Brown patients was graduating and had requested a sweat on the creek in his final days there. After Kenneth prepared and blessed the lodge, he told my sons they could come in with him before he started so he could tell them about it. They sat across from him while he explained what would happen in the lodge and what it was for; then he had me bring in some hot coals from the fire. He picked up a small red coal and put it in his mouth, rolled it around for a minute, spit it out and then told the boys that all things are possible with Grandfather and they had nothing to be afraid of as long as they stayed close to Grandfather and his teachings. He prayed for them and brushed them and himself with his eagle feather, leaving a trail of the blue glow over each of them. They have never forgotten that experience and have always gone to a sweat with Kenneth as often as they could. He told me later that he usually did not do those "hokey pokey tricks," but that Grandfather had told him it was ok to do it this once, so as to make an impression on the boys.

Almost every patient that graduated and left the Jack Brown Center wanted a Sweat Lodge Ceremony with their families as they were preparing to leave. At that time, family members came the week before discharge and stayed at the Center with their child, participating in their scheduled therapies and their graduation, which the patient planned with their counselors before the family members arrived. We also participated in the ceremonies the families brought and conducted as they welcomed their child back into their family and community. Kenneth often did specific healing ceremonies for the patients and it was there I learned how to use different ceremonies in the Sweat Lodge for healing different things.

At the same time I was learning from Kenneth and Rita, I was also seeking alternative methods to deal with my youngest son's attention deficit and became knowledgeable about what many consider "alternative medicine." I stayed in close counsel with Kenneth and Rita during this time because they wanted to be sure I did not get involved in any "new-age" scams that took advantage of people. They played an important role in how I have integrated alternative and Native healing in the things that I do to help others.

My husband died suddenly when my sons were 10 and 12. The Sweat Lodge was instrumental in our healing as a broken family and in helping my sons grow up to be strong men. As my oldest son reached the age of 16, he was struggling. We had moved back to Oklahoma City to be closer to family who could help me with them, and I wanted to do a maturity ceremony for him. I checked with the Cherokee medicine people I knew and they each told me that those ways had been lost a long time ago and they did not know how to direct me. So I talked with Kenneth and Rita and we devised a plan, using the Sweat Lodge, to create a ceremony for him. A group of us planned a ceremony at Kenneth's house where he had a Sweat Lodge in the backyard. My son planned for and collected items for his giveaway, told me who he wanted to invite and we set a spring date to hold it. It was a multi-tribal event. Counselors from the Jack Brown Center, who had watched my children grow up but who had all moved on to other jobs by then, attended our ceremony. One was Cherokee and agreed to give him a Cherokee name, and one was Pawnee who planned the breakfast feast. A Kiowa friend agreed to tend the rocks and keep the fire going all night, and others helped as well.

My son's ceremony began at sundown, with the rocks ready and everyone gathered. The first round was held with men, women, and relatives, with him coming in and sitting to the west, so he could see the fire when the door was open. We all told him what we appreciated about him and what we hoped for his future and what he could contribute to the world. We held the usual prayers and songs and then the round ended. The women and young people left the lodge then, and he stayed in with the men. These were the men who helped with the ceremony, the men he invited, and his male relatives. They talked to him about what it meant to be a man, how he should treat others, and how to be strong and stand up for himself in a good way. This group continued to the third round, but this time he talked about his hopes, dreams and fears and the man he wished to be as he got older. Then he was left alone in the lodge to spend the night thinking about what had been said, to pray about it, and to dream. The only person with him was the fire tender, keeping the fire going, but not talking with him.

During the remainder of the night attendees slept at local motels, in the house, or in campers they had driven down from their homes. At daylight, the men returned and went back in to complete the fourth and last round with him, to hear what he had learned and to hear about his plan for manhood. When they were done and ready to come out, all the people in the house were called down to the Sweat Lodge where we watched them come out one at a time, then Kenneth came out just ahead of him and presented him to the group, announcing he was now a man with a new name. His Cherokee name translated to Star Hunter and he proudly accepted a Pendleton blanket and an eagle feather from Kenneth. He then proceeded to thank everyone and gave each person a gift before we went to the house for the breakfast feast. This process was repeated for my youngest son a few years later. He was given the name of Big Bear at the ceremony. Both remember their ceremonies as one of the most memorable and life-changing events in their experience. My oldest son has taken his son to the Sweat Lodge and my youngest son recently had his young son blessed by Kenneth, just before his first birthday.

Since those memorable ceremonies for my songs, I have taken my young nephews into the sweat and they have had their health and personal issues addressed there. One nephew told me that in the sweat, "God came in and took out my heart, held it in his hands and then put it back in." They have all seen the blue glow and had extraordinary experiences. They also grew up loving going to Sweat Lodge Ceremonies and appreciating what it could do for them. Through Kenneth Coosewoon, my sons and members of my family have entered the Sweat Lodge and learned the blessings it can provide people.

Kenneth's healing abilities were by no means confined to the lodge, though. I once took him to see a friend of mine, who was also a nurse, while she was hospitalized with reflex sympathetic dystrophy (RSD), post a brown recluse spider bite. She called me after she was told her hand was going to have to be amputated due to the damage from the bite and resulting RSD. I called Kenneth and asked for help. He and Rita immediately came and we met at the hospital. Since Kenneth knew he could not burn cedar in the hospital, he burned it in the parking lot, waving his eagle feather through the smoke and praying for this person he had never met. He had made some prayer ties and a medicine bag for her. We went in to see her and her hand was totally black from necrosis and non-functional. We all prayed, Kenneth used his feather and gave her the prayer ties and medicine bag.

During our gathering at the hospital Kenneth said, "Grandfather says it is going to turn out alright; you should stay strong and believe." We left after about 20 minutes. The next day she called and said the surgery had been postponed, as she was improving. Several days passed and the surgery was totally cancelled. She no longer has RSD, but she still has her hand and full function of it to this day. As a result of Kenneth's prayers and the collective belief in the healing spirit of those gathered, my friend was healed and she was able to continue her journey and work on earth. This is just one story of many that has occurred over the years. Seemingly at every session I have attended with Kenneth Coosewoon, whether in the lodge or in a meeting, he has healed or helped someone. His commitment to help others through his medicine is remarkable.

Kenneth has also used the Sweat Lodge to help me teach my students from the University of Oklahoma College of Nursing. I once brought some undergraduate nursing students to a Sweat from the course I was teaching in obstetric nursing. In the lodge, Kenneth talked extensively to them about how the lodge is the womb of mother earth and that being inside of it is their chance to be reborn and renewed, to see the world with new eyes and to appreciate the light after being in the dark. Kenneth explained to the nursing students that they can be re-formed into whatever they want to be. They later told me that Kenneth's advice and their experience in the Sweat Lodge totally changed how they viewed pregnancy and birth. By entering the womb of the earth in the Sweat Lodge, the students explained that they now knew how to relate to the birthing experience personally.

After creating the Sweat Lodge, Kenneth takes a break in front of the holy space. Before each ceremony, Kenneth prepares by focusing his heart and mind on the ceremony ahead and how he can best help participants achieve the healing or advice they need to move forward in life in a positive, constructive manner.

Another time, we held a group session at a conference with a number of Native students. During the session, four different female students commented that they had been trying to get pregnant but had failed. They had expressed that they really wanted to start their families and were worried about why they could not seem to do so. Kenneth just listened, but as the session ended and he said goodbye to them, he also told them not to worry, as they would have good news soon. Each of those students became pregnant within the next couple of months. Some of these students had tried to get pregnant for more than two years, and had finally succeeded after participating in the Sweat Lodge Ceremony with Kenneth. When I related this, Kenneth just said, "well that's what I was told would happen." Kenneth has also helped many faculty members in the Sweat Lodge as they grappled with questions and issues from their life.

I continue to learn and grow in the medicine way with Kenneth and Rita's help, both having unique and special gifts to share. Kenneth has taught me the Sweat Lodge and helped me build my medicine box, contributing some of his medicine, feathers and other items of importance to healing. I, in turn, have shared what I know about other types of healing with him and have strived to help both Kenneth and Rita in any way that I can. We help each other on this journey through what Kenneth calls the "dead world," because true living and real life is where we are headed, to be reunited with our relatives and ancestors.

Conclusion

In our modern age, Kenneth Coosewoon's story has meaning. We live in a world of cynicism, materialism, and modernism, but Coosewoon's story speaks to hope, help, and healing. Most people grow up in a secular world, often devoid of the Spirit or an appreciation of their life's connection to the natural and spiritual world. And some churches preach the worthiness of a human to God based on a person's wealth, or canonize missionaries who incarcerated others and approved of whippings and other forms of corporal punishments. We have grown into a nation of self-satisfaction, ego, power, and money without great concern for plants, animals, places, and people. Too few people live in the service of others, caring about others or attempting to make the world a better place for all humanity and all life. Coosewoon's life provides a counter image to self and ego; not his entire life but most of his adult life.

For over forty years, Kenneth Coosewoon has followed the Good Red Road and employed his gift of healing and counseling for thousands of people. His life is an example of living a life in a good way, living a life for others. In his own humble way, Coosewoon is a leader of the healing community, by example, thought, word, and deed. Kenneth's story teaches us to care for each other and to love the earth, plants, animals, and natural world around them. This is not a new philosophy in world history but one not privileged enough today.

Coosewoon was born into the Comanche Nation of his father and the Kiowa Nation of his mother. He honors his family and people. Both sides of his family influenced his life, but as a young person, he gained only limited knowledge of his Indian identity and the spiritual and the medicinal background of his people. His family kept him separated from the spiritual side of his indigenous heritage, believing Kenneth would do better in the world without knowing or practicing the ancient beliefs about the Creator and His influence on man's activities on earth. As a boy Kenneth did not know that his Kiowa ancestors were medicine people, leaders of the Sweat Lodge who held ceremony on the very property where he grew up. His own grandfather was a ceremonial leader, but Kenneth had no idea that the old man and old woman led healing ceremonies. However, Kenneth grew up learning something of his ancestors and their great fighting ability. Coosewoon's Comanche and Kiowa ancestors were great warriors and hunters. This is equally so for Rita's ancestors. Their relatives fought enemies for generations, including Bluecoat Soldiers of the United States and volunteers made up of rangers composed of white settlers bent on killing every Comanche and Kiowa person in a concerted effort to exterminate Indians. Coosewoon's ancestors, and those of Rita Coosewoon, had earned respect and honor as superior warriors or as assistants to the warriors. Soldiers and settlers alike recognized the Comanche as great warriors, calling them the Lords of the Southern Plains.

By the twentieth century, those days of Comanche and Kiowa chasing enemies and buffalo across the prairies of present-day Oklahoma, Kansas, Texas, New Mexico, Colorado, and making raids into Mexico had long passed. The wars and open conflicts ended in the late nineteenth century, just a few generations before Kenneth's birth. By the time Kenneth was born, the old days were totally gone but not the deep culture of these Plains people. As one Native American scholar recently explained, "you can lose your car keys or your wallet, but you don't lose your culture." The deep and defining culture of the Comanche and Kiowa had changed but the people never lost their cultures. Life in the mid to late twentieth century changed dramatically for Native Americans of Oklahoma and the Southern Plains, but at the heart of the matter, the people retained essential elements of their cultures. Certainly the blood memory of Kenneth Coosewoon and Rita Coosewoon remained intact, perhaps latent but present as they journeyed through their lives. Times have changed throughout Indian Country during the twentieth and twenty-first centuries, but Kenneth retained within him the spark of life that made him uniquely Native, Comanche, and Kiowa.

As a young person, Kenneth heard many of those old stories about Comanche and Kiowa warriors, but he could not live like his ancestors. He grew up in a new era of great change, a time when American Indians were in transition from the old days and old ways to life in a modern world. He grew up in the 1940s and became an adult in the 1950s when the United States became a major world power. At the same time, Kenneth grew up in the Methodist Church in rural Oklahoma not far from his mother's home place. Kenneth never denigrated his mother's church or her choice to be Christian, but the religion did not speak to him. He spent his early years looking for something and trying to understand his place on earth. As a young person, Kenneth turned to sports, hunting, fishing, and riding horses. He had little concern about the world around him or the old Indian ways. However, as a young Native American, he wondered about his place within modern society, and without knowing it at the time, he wondered about his identity as a Native

American living in the twentieth century. In his own words, he reported that as a young man, he looked forward to having a good time, chasing beautiful women, owning a fancy car, and having money in his pocket.

When Kenneth entered college, he found joy in drinking and "being the big man on campus." When he was a young man, he cared little about learning about the spiritual life ways of his people or following a positive path that led him to sobriety. As a result, he followed a destructive road of alcohol and drugs that harmed his health, family, and future. He was usually able to function at a high level while drinking every day, but he reported, "something was always missing." Kenneth became an alcoholic and under the influence, he did foolish, even dangerous and illegal things. The deeper he got into the alcoholic pattern, the more he wondered why he could not be like other family men who found joy in life and family without alcohol. It was not until he hit rock bottom that he received a spiritual visitation telling him to change his ways and stop drinking so he could "live to wear out many blue jeans."

During his stay in the hospital recovering from far too much drink, the Little People and a Holy Spirit visited Kenneth. This visitation changed his life forever and began a series of spiritual encounters that continues today. In January 1974, Kenneth began walking the Good Red Road of sobriety, and he has followed this path ever since. Still, between 1974 and 1978, "something was missing" and Kenneth "kept trying to find out what was missing." In 1978, after four years of sobriety (four being a sacred number of Comanche and Kiowa people), Kenneth attended a gathering of drug and alcohol counselors working with Native American people. They met in the hill country of eastern Oklahoma, the home of Cherokee people. Wallace and Gracie Black Elk led the Sweat Lodge Ceremony for the various directors, including Kenneth Coosewoon, and during his tenure as "rock boy, tending the fire and the rocks used in the ceremony, Kenneth experienced the Great Vision and received Blue Medicine. The experiences led Kenneth down a path that revealed what had been missing in his life. He came

Rita Coosewoon is a healer in her own right and has helped hundreds of people. She is also a judge for the Comanche Nation and a professor of the Comanche language. In this photograph, Rita addresses students, staff, and faculty in the Costo Library of the University of California, Riverside.

face to face with Grandfather and instructions to heal people through the Sweat Lodge Ceremony. The Great Vision Kenneth received changed his life forever and the lives of thousands of people Kenneth has met, counseled, or healed.

For many readers, Kenneth's encounters with the Grandfather may seem far-fetched, a product of hallucinations brought on by alcohol and drugs. But to Kenneth and people that have worked with him, the visitations by holy entities, by spirits, were real and life changing, not hallucinations or figments of his imagination. They were real and true. The stories related by Kenneth Coosewoon fit well into patterns experienced over many centuries by Native American prophets, medicine people, and Indian doctors. His encounters with the spirit world are very much in line with the American Indian past and holy experiences of notable Native Americans. Most American Indian communities believe that certain individuals have and do experience direct contact with the spiritual world, and holy men and women have reported speaking to Grandfather, Creator, or Master of Life. Neolin, the Delaware Prophet, Tenskwatawa, the Shawnee Prophet, Kennekuk, the Kickapoo Prophet, Smohalla, the Washat Prophet, and Wovoka, the Paiute Prophet, are but a few of the medicine people who explained that they had direct contact with the Creator.

In addition, Lakota medicine man Black Elk, Cheyenne holy man Lame Deer, Apache man of power, Geronimo, and Lakota holy man Sitting Bull claimed to have gifts given to them of the most holy one, the supreme being. In the twentieth century, other Native Americans pointed out the Creator had given them the gift of healing, including Nez Perce/Palouse Andrew George, Mescalero Apache Paul Ortega, Cherokee Jim Henson, Cahuilla Ruby Modesto, Cherokee Croslin Smith, Wintu Florence Jones, and Lakota Wallace Black Elk. All of these Native Americans said they had spoken to the Creator or received divine messages. All of them had used their gift of healing to help other Native Americans. In the same way, Kenneth Coosewoon reported that the Creator or Grandfather had given him the power to heal others. But like other Native American healers, he was asked by the Creator to do his part in the healing but the final decision regarding the efficacy of a healing ceremony, prayers, or ritual depended on the Creator, not the medicine person.

174

During the Great Vision, Kenneth Coosewoon listened and learned. He reluctantly accepted the spiritual gifts and lessons taught him at Dwight Mission and acted on what he had learned. At first he did not feel deserving of such attention by the Creator, because Kenneth "had done every darn bad thing you could think of." But the Grandfather had chosen him to act on His behalf among the people and so Coosewoon took up the challenge and began to serve. He always emphasized to audiences, "if the Grandfather could forgive me for all the bad things I have done, then he will forgive you and give you good things to do on earth."

At Dwight Mission and afterwards, Kenneth learned to pray for others, and he has often told audiences and friends, "prayers are the most powerful things on earth but you have to believe and you have to ask." But the Grandfather, and not the medicine person, decides which prayers will be answered, but Kenneth says, "you must ask the Grandfather through prayer. You must pray, and ask for the health of others." As a result of the Great Vision, Kenneth began the life of a Native American healer, taking time with those in need and giving unselfishly of himself for the benefit of others.

In modern society, Coosewoon's life shines like a beacon for those searching for meaning in their lives and a better understanding of the human connection with the spiritual and natural world. During the first part of Kenneth's life, he journeyed through a fog searching for his life's meaning and his own identity. He had turned to temporal things, including alcohol, to make sense of his life but never found it. He was materialistic and ambivalent about Grandfather's creation of plants, animals, and places. But he learned. Kenneth has asked others to listen and learn.

He asks audiences today at schools, churches, universities, and various communities to seek their purpose in life. For many years, Kenneth walked in a fog not knowing who he was or what he should do on earth. His story mirrors that of hundreds, if not thousands of people, seeking meaning in their lives and a connection with the spiritual world. Coosewoon found his way through the fog and discovered the meaning of his life. Since 1974, he has tried to help other people from all walks of life understand their place and purpose on earth. Since 1978, he has healed many people with physical and mental ailments, through ancient Native American ways of healing and through his own common sense born of years of being alcoholic. Kenneth would say that when the Spirit offered to assist and teach him new ways, he was open to the teaching and began following a sacred path that he has shared with others.

During the second half of the twentieth century and early twenty-first century, many people have followed the shallow example of Rambo and Rocky, living their lives for their own self-gratification and selfish gain without concern for others. Coosewoon's life stands in marked contrast to materialism and secularism. Coosewoon has encouraged people he has "doctored" to live their lives in the Spirit with Grandfather at the center of their lives. He has asked them to trust in Grandfather for guidance and to believe that the Creator will provide for them so they might know more and be able to help others. When Kenneth speaks before large audiences, he never preaches but asks people to consider a life of giving and helping others. He asks that people turn their back on self-satisfaction, selfishness, ego, and materialism.

Coosewoon's life is an example of following this spiritual path and trusting in the Creator. His life has transcended the self. He has lived out his creed to live in the Spirit and help others—not for fame and fortune. After the Great Vision and his acceptance of Blue Medicine, Kenneth Coosewoon learned the Sweat Lodge Ceremony. After the Great Vision, he began to follow the holy instructions given to him by Grandfather. He also trusted that Grandfather would be true to his word and always be with him. Kenneth believed Grandfather would help him, guiding him throughout his life until he wore out his last pair of blue jeans.

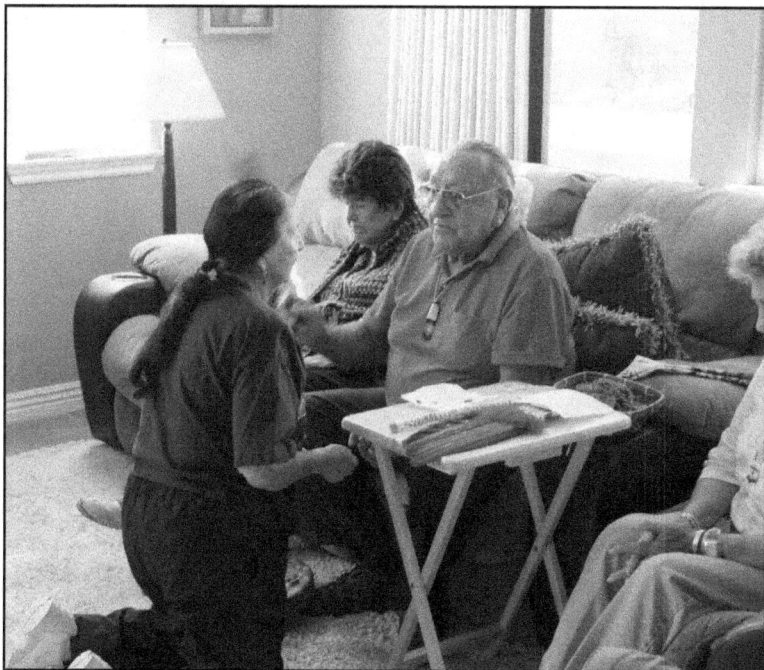

Kenneth is shown here during a healing ceremony in which he blessed several individuals of varying ages, including Mrs. Lofton (seated to the right of Kenneth), a Luiseño tribal elder from the La Jolla Indian Reservation. The photograph was taken at the home of Bill and Monica Madrigal in Southern California.

The Native American Student Association of the University of California, Riverside, hosts the annual Medicine Ways Conference. Kenneth and Rita Coosewoon participate in the conference, providing lectures and assistance to those seeking healing. They are pictured here singing the Calling Song.

In a secular age, Coosewoon's life provides an example of a life well lived for the benefit of others. His example points the way for others. He urges people to follow their bliss but remember to be of help to others. He tells individuals and groups to listen for the quiet messages that can come to human beings when they take the time to listen and follow a path of service. Kenneth explained that

Grandfather has a specific purpose for every life, and that people may find that purpose through prayer, ceremony, and healing. Kenneth believes that every person has a holy purpose on earth and may find their correct path by praying and following the positive path of service for others. He knows that many people struggled early in life attempting to find their way and overcome challenges. Many people have to overcome physical, mental, and sexual abuse or the horrors of poverty, alienation, alcohol, and drug addiction. These are the people that need help the most, but he also has reached out to men, women, and children that seem to have the world at their feet. Coosewoon believes that many young people seek to find the right path to follow and to understand their place in the modern world. His life is a lesson for them, and at meetings at schools, colleges, and universities, Coosewoon uses his own life experiences to help young people find their way.

For many years, Kenneth Coosewoon has spent a good deal of time helping young children at the San Marcos Treatment Center in Texas. At least twice a year, Kenneth has run a Sweat Lodge Ceremony for the children, taking them into the ceremonial lodge to discuss their problems and allowing the children to offer prayers of healing for themselves and others. There, Kenneth has found some of the purist prayers of love and concern for others that he has ever encountered. Kenneth has helped the children find their purpose in life, in spite of their physical or mental problems. His ceremonies at the San Marcos Treatment Center and beyond have touched the lives of hundreds of young people, and his work among the young people at San Marcos and many other sites has enriched his own life, enlarging his ability to help others in a positive, meaningful manner.

For many years, Kenneth Coosewoon has presented his philosophy to large crowds of Indians and non-Indians at the annual Medicine Ways Conference at the University of California, Riverside. Coosewoon has spoken to huge crowds of people, so many attending that the organizers have had to find larger spaces for his presentations. Each year, more people attend the conference primarily to hear Kenneth speak, and some have asked him to help them with their physical and mental problems. At one such gathering alone, Kenneth prayed for a Lakota woman who needed a new liver and another woman who had cancer. The Lakota woman did not have to have a liver transplant, and the other young woman witnessed her cancer go into remission and remain in remission for over four years. He prayed for another young woman with stage four cancer and the disease disappeared. The following year, the woman presented Kenneth with her newborn baby, a gift given by Grandfather and testament to the Healing Spirit. During the Great Vision, Grandfather promised Kenneth that he would "witness many miracles," and Coosewoon points out that at least three of these miracles took place at the Medicine Ways Conference.

As of this writing, Kenneth Coosewoon is in semi-retirement. He lives with his grandson, Ron Cooper and Ron's wife, Kristal, at his home in Medicine Park, Oklahoma, where he tends to his home place, reads books, and watches the Oklahoma City Thunder play winning basketball games. He still enjoys sports and telephone calls from family and friends. Kenneth and Rita remain open to helping other people through the Sweat Lodge Ceremony, but they no longer travel great distances or enter the prisons. But Kenneth and Rita are both available to pray for healing, which they do for others. Kenneth receives letters from friends asking for healing prayers for those in need, and he is always open to help those willing to put their faith into the hands of Grandfather and remember to act in harmony with Grandfather. At the end of his prayer, Kenneth recalls the words of his Lakota teachers and remembers, "All My Relations."

About The Authors

Clifford E. Trafzer is Distinguished Professor of History, Rupert Costo Chair in American Indian Affairs, and Director of the California Center for Native Nations at the University of California, Riverside. A man of Wyandot and German descent, he has recently published *A Chemehuevi Song: Resiliency of a Southern Paiute Tribe* (University of Washington Press, 2015) and *River Song: Naxiyamt'ama (Snake River-Palouse) Oral Traditions from Mary Jim, Andrew George, Gordon Fisher, and Emily Peone* (Washington State University Press, 2015) with Richard D. Scheuerman.

Beverly Patchell is a citizen of the Cherokee Nation and Assistant Professor of Nursing at the University of Utah. She earned her B.S. in Nursing and M.S. in Psychiatric Mental Health Nursing at the University of Oklahoma Health Sciences Center in Oklahoma City. In 2011, the Regents of New Mexico State University awarded her the Ph. D. in Nursing with significant research, "American Indian Adolescents Response to a Culturally Tailored Substance Abuse Prevention Intervention." She has published in the *Journal of Cultural Diversity, Journal of Theory Construction and Testing,* and *Advances in Nursing Science.* For many years, she directed the American Indian Nursing Program at the University of Oklahoma Health Science Center.

Ronald R. Cooper is a member of the Comanche Nation and author of *It's My Trail, Too: A Comanche Indian's Journey on the Cherokee Trail of Tears* (Lakeside, Arizona: www.createspace.com). Since his youth, Cooper has followed the teachings of his Grandfather, Kenneth Coosewoon, conducting ceremonies and healing others through the Sweat Lodge. For many years, Cooper worked at various National Parks throughout the United States with his wife, Kristal D. Cooper. With the support of Kristal, Ronald walked the Trail of Tears National Historic Trail to bring awareness of the "despair of this event and tragedies like it throughout Native American history."

www.ingramcontent.com/pod-product-compliance
Lightning Source LLC
LaVergne TN
LVHW051051080426
835508LV00019B/1814